Kaplan Publishing are constantly finding new ways to make a difference to ~~your~~ exciting online resources rea~~dy and something~~ different to students looking ~~for exam success.~~

D1151943

This book comes with free MyKaplan online resources so that you can study anytime, anywhere. **This free online resource is not sold separately and is included in the price of the book.**

Having purchased this book, you have access to the following online study materials:

CONTENT	AAT	
	Text	Kit
Electronic version of the book		
Progress tests with instant answers		
Mock assessments online		
Material updates		

How to access your online resources

Kaplan Financial students will already have a MyKaplan ~~account and th~~ ~~resources will be available to you online. You do not need to register again, as this p~~ ~~was co~~ ~~when you enrolled. If you are having problems accessing online materials, please as~~

If you are not studying with Kaplan and did not pu~~rchase your b~~ ~~website, to unlock your extra online resources please go to www.mykaplan.co.uk/addabc~~ ~~an account and registered books previously). You will then need to enter the ISBN num~~ ~~back cover) and the unique pass key number contained in the scratch panel below to gain~~ ~~equired to enter additional information during this process to set up or confirm your acc~~

If you purchased through Kaplan Flexible Lear~~ning~~ ~~Publishing~~ website you will automatically receive an e-mail invitation to MyKaplan. Please register ~~your~~ ~~this~~ email to gain access to your content. If you do not receive the e-mail or book content, please con~~tact Kaplan Publishing.~~

Your Code and Information

This code can only be used once for the registration of one book online. This registration and your online content will expire when the final sittings for the examinations covered by this book have taken place. Please allow one hour from the time you submit your book details for us to process your request.

ST029135

CORNWALL COLLEGE

Please scratch the film to access your MyKaplan code.

Please be aware that this code is case-sensitive and you will need to include the dashes within the passcode, but not when entering the ISBN. For further technical support, please visit www.MyKaplan.co.uk

KAPLAN
PUBLISHING

AAT

AQ2016

FOUNDATION CERTIFICATE IN ACCOUNTING

Synoptic Assessment

EXAM KIT

This Exam Kit supports study for the following AAT qualifications:

AAT Foundation Certificate in Accounting – Level 2

AAT Foundation Diploma in Accounting and Business – Level 2

AAT Foundation Certificate in Bookkeeping – Level 2

AAT Foundation Award in Accounting Software – Level 2

AAT Level 2 Award in Accounting Skills to Run Your Business

AAT Foundation Certificate in Accounting at SCQF Level 5

Kaplan Feedback
Tell us what you think

KAPLAN

PUBLISHING

British Library Cataloguing-in-Publication Data

A catalogue record for this book is available from the British Library.

Published by:

Kaplan Publishing UK

Unit 2 The Business Centre

Molly Millar's Lane

Wokingham

Berkshire

RG41 2QZ

ISBN: 978-1-78740-004-7

© Kaplan Financial Limited, 2017

Printed and bound in Great Britain.

CONTENTS

Features in this exam kit

In addition to providing a wide ranging bank of real exam style questions, we have also included in this kit:

- unit-specific information and advice on exam technique

- our recommended approach to make your revision for this particular unit as effective as possible.

You will find a wealth of other resources to help you with your studies on the AAT website:

www.aat.org.uk/

Quality and accuracy are of the utmost importance to us so if you spot an error in any of our products, please send an email to mykaplanreporting@kaplan.com with full details, or follow the link to the feedback form in MyKaplan.

Our Quality Co-ordinator will work with our technical team to verify the error and take action to ensure it is corrected in future editions.

SYNOPTIC ASSESSMENT

AAT AQ16 introduces a Synoptic Assessment, which students must complete if they are to achieve the appropriate qualification upon completion of a qualification. In the case of the Foundation Certificate in Accounting, students must pass all of the mandatory assessments and the Synoptic Assessment to achieve the qualification.

As a Synoptic Assessment is attempted following completion of individual units, it draws upon knowledge and understanding from those units. It may be appropriate for students to retain their study materials for individual units until they have successfully completed the Synoptic Assessment for that qualification.

All units within the Foundation Certificate in Accounting are mandatory. Four units are assessed individually in end of unit assessments, but this qualification also includes a synoptic assessment, sat towards the end of the qualification, which draws on and assesses knowledge and understanding from across the qualification.

- Bookkeeping Transactions – end of unit assessment
- Bookkeeping Controls – end of unit assessment
- Elements of Costing – end of unit assessment
- Work Effectively in Finance – assessed within the synoptic assessment only

Note that Using Accounting Software is a unit assessment only and is not assessed as part of the synoptic assessment. Note also that Work Effectively in Finance is assessed in the synoptic assessment only.

Summary of learning outcomes from underlying units which are assessed in the synoptic assessment

Underlying unit	Learning outcomes required
Work Effectively in Finance	LO1, LO2, LO3, LO4
Bookkeeping Transactions	LO2, LO3, LO4, LO5
Bookkeeping Controls	LO3, LO4, LO5
Elements of Costing	LO2, LO3

FORMAT OF THE ASSESSMENT

The specimen synoptic assessment comprises seven tasks and covers all four assessment objectives. Students will be assessed by computer-based assessment. Marking of the assessment is partially by computer and partially human marked.

In any one assessment, students may not be assessed on all content, or on the full depth or breadth of a piece of content. The content assessed may change over time to ensure validity of assessment, but all assessment criteria will be tested over time.

The synoptic assessment will ask students to apply knowledge and skills gained across the qualification in an integrated way, within a workplace context. Scenarios will change over time to ensure the validity of the assessment.

The following weighting is based upon the AAT Qualification Specification documentation which may be subject to variation.

	Assessment objective	Weighting
AO1	Demonstrate an understanding of the finance function and the roles and procedures carried out by members of an accounting team	24%
AO2	Process transactions, complete calculations and make journal entries	24%
AO3	Compare, produce and reconcile journals and accounts	34%
AO4	Communicate financial information effectively	18%
	Total	100%

Time allowed

2 hours

PASS MARK

The pass mark for all AAT assessments is 70%.

 Always keep your eye on the clock and make sure you attempt all questions!

DETAILED SYLLABUS

The detailed syllabus and study guide written by the AAT can be found at:

www.aat.org.uk/

ASSESSMENT OBJECTIVES

The synoptic assessment objectives are based upon the learning outcomes of four of the units which are subject to individual unit assessment. Note that not all of the content of those units is assessable in the synoptic assessment. Note also that content from Using Accounting Software is not part of the assessment objective.

To perform this synoptic assessment effectively you will need to know and understand the following:

Assessment objective 1	Demonstrate an understanding of the finance function and the roles and procedures carried out by members of an accounting team
Related learning outcomes	**Work Effectively in Finance** LO1 Understand the finance function within an organisation LO2 Use personal skills development in finance LO3 Produce work effectively LO4 Understand corporate social responsibility (CSR), ethics and sustainability within organisations
Assessment objective 2	Process transactions complete calculations and make journal entries
Related learning outcomes	**Bookkeeping transactions** LO2 Process customer transactions LO3 Process supplier transactions LO4 Process receipts and payments LO5 Process transactions through the ledgers to the trial balance
Assessment objective 3	Compare, produce and reconcile journals and accounts
Related learning outcomes	**Bookkeeping Controls** LO3 Use control accounts LO4 Use the journal LO5 Reconcile a bank statement with the cash book **Elements of Costing** LO2 Use cost recording techniques LO3 Provide information on actual and budgeted costs and income
Assessment objective 4	Communicate financial information effectively
Related learning outcome	**Work Effectively in Finance** LO3 Produce work effectively

INDEX TO QUESTIONS AND ANSWERS

EXAM TECHNIQUE

- **Do not skip any of the material** in the syllabus.

- **Read each question** *very* carefully.

- **Double-check your answer** before committing yourself to it.

- Answer **every** question – if you do not know an answer to a multiple choice question or true/false question, you don't lose anything by guessing. Think carefully before you **guess**.

- If you are answering a multiple-choice question, **eliminate first those answers that you know are wrong.** Then choose the most appropriate answer from those that are left.

- **Don't panic** if you realise you've answered a question incorrectly. Getting one question wrong will not mean the difference between passing and failing.

Computer-based exams – tips

- Do not attempt a CBA until you have **completed all study material** relating to it.

- On the AAT website there is a CBA demonstration. It is **ESSENTIAL** that you attempt this before your real CBA. You will become familiar with how to move around the CBA screens and the way that questions are formatted, increasing your confidence and speed in the actual exam.

- Be sure you understand how to use the **software** before you start the exam. If in doubt, ask the assessment centre staff to explain it to you.

- Questions are **displayed on the screen** and answers are entered using keyboard and mouse. At the end of the exam, in the case of those units not subject to human marking, you are given a certificate showing the result you have achieved.

- In addition to the traditional multiple-choice question type, CBAs will also contain **other types of questions**, such as number entry questions, drag and drop, true/false, pick lists or drop down menus or hybrids of these.

- In some CBAs you will have to type in complete computations or written answers.

- You need to be sure you **know how to answer questions** of this type before you sit the exam, through practice.

KAPLAN'S RECOMMENDED REVISION APPROACH

QUESTION PRACTICE IS THE KEY TO SUCCESS

Success in professional examinations relies upon you acquiring a firm grasp of the required knowledge at the tuition phase. In order to be able to do the questions, knowledge is essential.

However, the difference between success and failure often hinges on your exam technique on the day and making the most of the revision phase of your studies.

The **Kaplan Study Text** is the starting point, designed to provide the underpinning knowledge to tackle all questions. However, in the revision phase, poring over text books is not the answer.

Kaplan Pocket Notes are designed to help you quickly revise a topic area; however you then need to practise questions. There is a need to progress to exam style questions as soon as possible, and to tie your exam technique and technical knowledge together.

The importance of question practice cannot be over-emphasised.

The recommended approach below is designed by expert tutors in the field, in conjunction with their knowledge of the examiner and the specimen assessment.

You need to practise as many questions as possible in the time you have left.

OUR AIM

Our aim is to get you to the stage where you can attempt exam questions confidently, to time, in a closed book environment, with no supplementary help (i.e. to simulate the real examination experience).

Practising your exam technique is also vitally important for you to assess your progress and identify areas of weakness that may need more attention in the final run up to the examination.

In order to achieve this we recognise that initially you may feel the need to practice some questions with open book help.

Good exam technique is vital.

THE KAPLAN REVISION PLAN

Stage 1: Assess areas of strengths and weaknesses

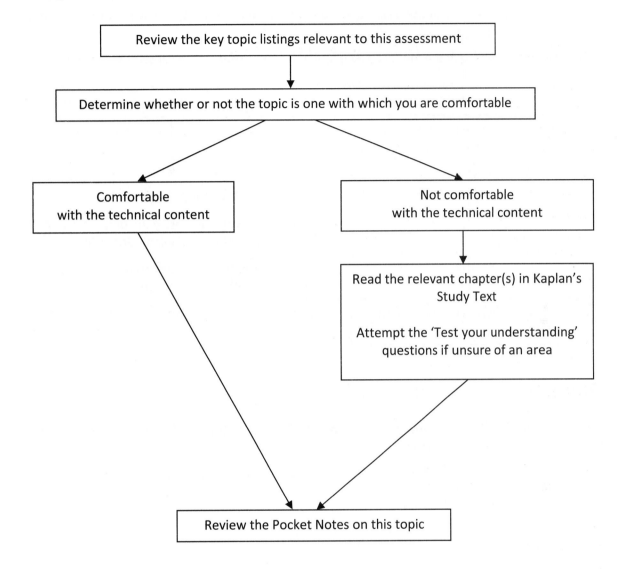

Stage 2: Practice questions

Follow the order of revision of topics as presented in this Kit and attempt the questions in the order suggested.

Try to avoid referring to Study Texts and your notes and the model answer until you have completed your attempt.

Review your attempt with the model answer and assess how much of the answer you achieved.

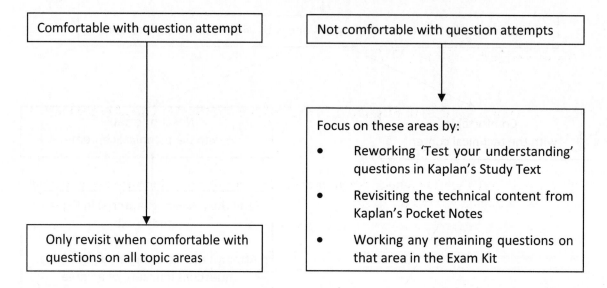

| Comfortable with question attempt | Not comfortable with question attempts |

Focus on these areas by:

- Reworking 'Test your understanding' questions in Kaplan's Study Text
- Revisiting the technical content from Kaplan's Pocket Notes
- Working any remaining questions on that area in the Exam Kit

Only revisit when comfortable with questions on all topic areas

Stage 3: Final pre-exam revision

We recommend that you **attempt at least one mock examination** containing a set of previously unseen exam-standard questions.

Attempt the mock CBA online in timed, closed book conditions to simulate the real exam experience.

Section 1

PRACTICE QUESTIONS

ASSESSMENT OBJECTIVE 1

LO1 UNDERSTAND THE FINANCE FUNCTION WITHIN AN ORGANISATION

1   POLICIES AND PROCEDURES

Select THREE policies and procedures from the following list which are likely to apply to the accounting function:

A   Data Protection Act

B   Health and Safety at Work

C   Curriculum policy

D   Authorised signatory procedure

E   Kitchen Hygiene policy

F   Administration of substances policy

2   DOCUMENTS

The accounts department of an organisation receives documents and information from other departments.

Match the department with the ONE document they would send to the accounts department:

Department	Document
Purchasing Department	(a) Bank interest charged
	(b) Copy of Purchase order
HR Department	(c) Sales Commission
	(d) New employee forms
Payroll Department	(e) Statutory Sick pay forms
	(f) Customer invoice

3   DEPARTMENTS

Match the following departments to ONE information type it would normally use:

Department	Information
Sales Dept	Health and Safety guidelines.
Accounts Dept	List of all new employees for the period.
Payroll Dept	Cheque book stubs.
	Commission payable to sales staff.
	Employee car registration numbers.

4   PRINCIPLES

Select THREE principles from the list below that are not a part of the Data Protection Act 1998.

- Data processed fairly and lawfully.
- Information obtained for personal use.
- Historic information that is not up to date.
- Not kept longer than necessary.
- Transferred to other countries without authorisation.

5   DATA SECURITY

(a)   **Which ONE item would be the best method to back up data from your computer?**

- printing out paper copies of everything and filing them away
- make a copy on a removable storage device e.g. DVD, external hard drive
- keep a second copy of the data on your hard disk

(b)   **Where should data back-ups from your computer be kept?**

- in a separate locked room or off site
- in a drawer near the computer
- on the computer's hard disk

(c)   **Which ONE of the following is less likely to damage or delete data?**

- archiving
- a virus
- system breakdown

(d)   **State three features of a secure password.**

- Feature 1
- Feature 2
- Feature 3

(e)   **Which ONE of the following is not a physical control to protect data?**

- Restricting access to an office
- Installing an alarm system
- Passwords

6   INFORMATION

(a)   **Identify the FOUR key characteristics of useful information from the list below:**

- understandable
- accurate
- legible
- complete
- timely
- credible
- fit for purpose

(b)   **Identify whether each of the following statements is TRUE or FALSE.**

- Only information stated in monetary terms is useful to accountants

– True/False

- Non-financial information is useful information to individuals who make decisions

– True/False

7   SERVICE PROVISION

Which TWO of the following services are staff in the finance function most likely to provide to staff in the sales department?

- Conducting job interviews
- Preparing sales brochures
- Budget report analysis
- Photocopier servicing
- Marketing new products
- Payment of sales commission

8   STAKEHOLDERS

Identify which TWO of the following stakeholders a trainee in the finance function is most likely to communicate with.

- People living in houses close to the organisation's Head Office
- The local MP
- H M Revenue & Customs
- The Head teacher of the local school
- Receivables
- An AAT examiner

9   REPORTING LINES

A business employs 2 Directors, 3 Managers and 6 Assistants.

Identify who each person should report to by selecting from the picklist. You may use an item more than once.

Person	Should report to the following
Sales and Purchase Ledger Assistant	
Administration Assistant	
3 Sales Assistants	
Payroll Assistant	
Accounting Department Manager	

Picklist: Managing director, Finance director, Sales manager, Accounts department manager, General manager

10   PERSON AND ROLE

Match which ONE person each role must report to:

Role

Accounts assistant

Sales Ledger clerk

Machine operator

Reports to

Payroll manager

Finance director

HR manager

Factory manager

Accounting department manager

Marketing assistant

11   COMPLIANCE AND SOLVENCY

Select TWO actions that will ensure the legal compliance and two actions that will help the solvency of a business

Action	Legal Compliance	Solvency
Ensure financial statements are filed on time.		
Improve credit control procedures.		
Maintain a petty cash book.		
Create and maintain a cash budget.		
Ensure the work place is a safe environment for staff and visitors.		

12   THE ACCOUNTING FUNCTION

The Accounting function is an essential part of the business.

Select TWO actions for each of the columns. Actions should only be selected once:

Actions	Efficient running of the business	Solvency of the business	Legal Compliance
Monitor cashflow.			
Provide quotation to customer.			
Ensure Sales Tax is paid to HMRC on time.			
Regularly chase outstanding receivables.			
Ensure inventory is ordered when it falls to the minimum level.			
Ensure members of staff are first aid trained.			
Regular maintenance of machinery.			
Produce a staff rota for tea making.			

13   ISSUES

Some issues should be referred to a manager if they are unable to be resolved easily by an employee.

Which TWO of the following issues would you try to resolve yourself?

- The paper for the photocopier keeps running out without a new order being placed.

- You suspect a colleague is being harassed by another colleague.

- Your manager has requested you complete a task you do not have sufficient knowledge to complete.

- Somebody in the office continues to prop the fire door open.

14   PETTY CASH

Identify the most likely effect on the organisation if you were unable to complete the petty cash reconciliation on time.

- Your colleagues would be unable to complete their work on time.

- Fraudulent activity may have taken place and go undetected.

- Petty cash will be withdrawn, replaced with invoicing for small purchases.

15   CONFLICT

Some issues may lead to conflict in the workplace.

Indicate which issues can be resolved by you and which should be referred to your line manager.

Issue	Resolve myself	Refer to line manager
Your manager has asked you to complete a Statement of Financial position; however you do not have the accounting knowledge to do this.		
You suspect your colleague knows your computer password.		
You suspect an expenses form which has been passed to you has non-business expenses on it and the form has been submitted by a manager.		

LO2 USE PERSONAL SKILLS DEVELOPMENT IN FINANCE

16   CPD

(a)   **Identify TWO of the following activities that count towards an employee's Continuing Professional Development requirements.**

- Attend a client lunch meeting to discuss improving services offered.

- Complete a course to further relevant knowledge.

- Arrive at work one hour earlier every day during busy times.

- Read articles online related to the trade in which the employee works.

(b)   **Identify the Strength, Weakness, Opportunity and Threat from the information listed below.**

	Strength	Weakness	Opportunity	Threat
Attend a time management course.				
Leaves filing to the end of the week.				
Excellent customer service.				
Insufficient staff members to cover time off for courses.				

17 PERFORMANCE

Your manager has reviewed your performance over the past 6 months and the following has been noted.

Strengths	*Weaknesses*
Excellent computer skills.	Lack of confidence with clients.
Enthusiasm for learning.	Little double entry knowledge.

Indicate which TWO courses would be appropriate for you to attend:

- Bookkeeping course.
- Online computer studies course.
- Communication and presentation skills.
- Nail art evening classes.
- Kick boxing classes.

Identify whether each of the following statements is TRUE or FALSE.

A qualified accountant does not need to attend Continued Professional Development courses   – True/False

CPD must be undertaken for a minimum of 1 day per month   – True/False

18 WEAKNESSES

(a)   Your manager has assessed that you have the following weaknesses:

   (1)   Poor communications skills.

   (2)   Poor timekeeping.

   (3)   Inadequate technical accounting skills.

   Which of the following 3 courses of action could address each of the weaknesses identified?

   - Attend a bookkeeping course.
   - Learn to drive.
   - Buy new accounting software.
   - Adopt a new clock in and out system for the office.
   - Attend a 'how to communicate in an office' course.
   - Go on a sky dive course.

(b)   **Identify whether each of the following statements is TRUE or FALSE.**

   All accountants, qualified and unqualified must complete CPD   – True/False

   CPD must be carried out on an annual basis by unqualified members   – True/False

   CPD must be carried out on an annual basis by qualified members   – True/False

19   APPRAISAL

Identify whether each of the following statements is TRUE or FALSE.

An employee performance appraisal is designed to focus solely upon weaknesses problems experienced by an employee during the appraisal period.   – True/False

There is a benefit in an employee undertaking a self-appraisal exercise even if their employer operates a system of annual appraisal.   – True/False

An appraisal is a 'backward looking process' that concentrates solely upon what has happened during the previous year.   – True/False

An appraisal process should allow an employee the opportunity to identify and discuss aspects of their work that they have either performed very well or performed less well during the previous year.   – True/False

An effective appraisal process should result in objectives or goals to be achieved during the following year.   – True/False

20   SELF-DEVELOPMENT

You currently work in the financial accounting department of your organisation and have identified the need for some self-development activities.

Identify the development activity from the picklist below that will help you to meet each of your self-development needs.

Self-development need	Development activity
To improve your practical experience of using the purchase ledger management system used by your organisation	
To develop a better understanding of financial accounting theory, principles and techniques	
To improve your knowledge of the goods and services provided by your organisation	
To improve your knowledge and understanding of how the management accounting department compiles product costings	
To improve your communication and presentation skills in meetings	

Picklist: Study for a professional accountancy qualification, Attend practical course, Secondment to another department, Product catalogue review, Work shadowing,

LO3 PRODUCE WORK EFFECTIVELY

21   (a)   REGIONAL SALES

Regional sales made by a business for the three months ended 31 March 20X2 were as follows:

Eastern region	£200,000
Western region	£180,000
South	£150,000
North	£160,000

(a)   **What was the total sales figure for the quarter?**

(b)   **What percentage of the total sales was made by the North (round your answer to 2 decimal places)?**

(c)   **What percentage of total sales was made by the Eastern and Western regions (round your answer to 2 decimal places)?**

(b)   WIGGINS LTD

Below are the sales figures of Wiggins Limited for the six months ended 31 August 20X4:

20X4	Sales – (£)
March	456,123
April	459,578
May	461,591
June	465,837
July	468,149
August	472,298

(a)   **What were the total sales for the first 3 months?**

(b)   **What was the percentage increase from March to April?**

(c)   **What will sales be in September 20X4 if they are 5% higher than August 20X4?**

(d)   **How much higher (in £) are sales in June than March?**

Note: (round all answers to 2 decimal places).

22   BOB

You are the manager of an accountancy firm (bob – bob@accountancyfirm.co.uk)

You want to discuss the exam performance of the AAT trainees with the training manager, Ally Mckoist (ally@accountancyfirm.co.uk). One student in particular (John Barnes) has performed poorly.

Please complete this email by selected from the drop down lists and filling the blanks:

From: bob@accountancyfirm.co.uk

To: _____

Subject: **(Hello/Discussion/AAT feedback/AAT Exam Performance)**

Hello Ally,

I would like to discuss the above with you **(now/whenever/tomorrow afternoon)**. In particular I would like to review the performance of **(Johnboy/Jimsy/John Barnes)** with a view to finding out why he has performed **(poorly/so well/good)**. I also hope we can resolve this issue by **(threatening John with the sack/working together with John/sending him an email)**.

Regards

Bob

23   K KIPLING

Complete the e-mail shown below, which is confirming an appointment with a client Mr K Kipling (kk@cakes4tea.org.uk) to take place at his premises on Monday at 2.30 pm to discuss the business plan for the forthcoming year with Mrs Anna Howes.

From: AATstudent@Kaplan.co.uk

To: _____

Subject: **(Meeting request, meeting confirmation, telephone call)**

Good Morning Mr Kipling

Following our telephone conversation I confirm the meeting which is to take place at **(your home/your premises/your bank)** on **(Saturday/Sunday/Monday/Tuesday)** at **(12.30 pm/1.30 pm/2 pm/2.30 pm/3 pm)**.

I will bring a copy of the business plan I have prepared.

Kind regards

(Ann Howes

Anna How

Anna Howes)

24 JOSHUA VALENTINE

The following is a partially completed email to inform Joshua Valentine (jvalentine@atoz.org.uk), Carmel Jenton (cjenton@atoz.org.uk) and Dane Wheeler (dwheeler@atoz.org.uk) of a conference on Thursday at 10am in the King's Hotel. The conference is being held to cover the issue of recycling within organisations. **Please complete as appropriate.**

From:	AATstudent@atoz.org.uk
To:	_____
	_____
Subject:	_____

Hello All,

This conference is being held at _____ on _____ at _____am.

The conference will be held regarding the issue of recycling within organisations.

Please confirm your attendance.

Regards,

AAT Student

25 WORK SCHEDULE

Below is your work scheduled to be completed this week. You work part time from 8 am to 4 pm Monday to Wednesday and you have an hour for lunch at 12.30 pm. There is the weekly planning meeting on Monday at 8.15 am which lasts for 45 minutes.

You routine tasks for the week are:

Daily

Open and distribute the post	9 am (takes 1 hour)
Frank post and take to the post office	3.30 pm (takes 30 mins)

Monday

Process Sales invoices onto Sage	10 am (takes 1 hr 30 mins)

Tuesday

Process Purchase invoices onto Sage	10.30 pm (takes 1 hr 30 mins)

Wednesday

Prepare bank and petty cash reconciliations	1 hour

You have been requested to assist the Payroll Manager on Monday afternoon to calculate the Salesmen's bonuses for the period which must be processed on Tuesday at 2 pm to ensure these are paid at the end of the week.

Complete your to-do list for Monday in order of task completion.

(1)

(2)

(3)

(4)

(5)

26   WORK PLANNING

Your workload for the coming week is shown below. You work from 9am to 5pm and take a lunch break from 12:30 – 1:30pm every day.

Task	Tasks to be completed by:		Task Duration
	Day	Time	
Process payroll.	Friday	11am	2 hrs
Bank reconciliations.	Every day	4.30pm	1 hr
Wages reconciliation.	Thursday	2pm	3 hrs
Overtime calculation.	Wednesday	12pm	2 hrs
Team meeting.	Thursday	10am	1 hr
Cash to bank.	Every day	5pm	½ hr

You receive the following email from your line manager on Wednesday at 5pm:

Hi,

Tomorrow I will be leaving the office at 3pm to meet a potential new customer. I will need to check the wages reconciliation before I go so that the staff are paid on Friday.

Thanks

Tomorrow is Thursday. Please list the order in which you are to complete these tasks:

Process payroll	(1st, 2nd, 3rd, 4th, 5th, 6th)
Bank reconciliation	(1st, 2nd, 3rd, 4th, 5th, 6th)
Wages reconciliation	(1st, 2nd, 3rd, 4th, 5th, 6th)
Overtime calculation	(1st, 2nd, 3rd, 4th, 5th, 6th)
Team meeting	(1st, 2nd, 3rd, 4th, 5th, 6th)
Cash to bank	(1st, 2nd, 3rd, 4th, 5th, 6th)

27 FEEDBACK

50 feedback forms have been sent out by e-mail to the delegates following a training course. The results are shown in the table below:

Question	Response Yes	Response No
Was the course content relevant to your job role?	15	5
Did the presenter explain the purpose of the training?	20	1
Would you recommend the course to others?	18	2
Was the venue easy to find?	6	15

Select TWO conclusions from the list below that could be drawn from the feedback:

- The course was not relevant to the delegates' job role.

- Most delegates found the venue difficult to find.

- The course was not very successful.

- The course was relevant to the delegates' job role.

Select TWO items from the list below which should be investigated:

- Why did we send the staff on the course?

- Why was there so little feedback received?

- Look for a different venue.

- Do we need to use a different presenter?

28 SURVEY

The following survey was recently carried out at a company.

	Number of staff that agreed	Number of staff that disagreed	Number of staff that did not answer
Are you happy with your work/life balance?	12	45	3
Are you satisfied with your current pay?	34	24	2
Do you believe you have strong promotion prospects in your current role?	5	55	0

(a) **How many people were asked each question?**

(b) **In terms of work/life balance, are staff happy/unhappy?**

(c) **In terms of current pay/are most people happy/unhappy?**

(d) **Do the majority of people agree that there are good promotion prospects – yes/no?**

29   REPORT CONTENT

What information is usually contained within the areas of a report listed below?

	Introduction	Appendices
Information regarding what the report is based upon.		
Supporting calculations for figures contained within the body of the report.		

LO4 CORPORATE SOCIAL RESPONSIBILITY, ETHICS AND SUSTAINABILITY

30   PRINCIPLES

The fundamental code of ethics set out five principles that a professional accountant is required to comply with. Two principles are objectivity and professional competence/due care.

Select TWO other ethical principles from the list below.

A   Confidence

B   Integrity

C   Truthfulness

D   Confidentiality

31   COMPANY SHARES

Your father owns some shares in a company which your company audits. You have recently found out that the company is struggling. This is going to be announced publicly shortly and will have an adverse effect on the share price.

Which TWO fundamental ethical principles prevent you from telling your father about this?

A   Confidentiality

B   Objectivity

C   Professional Behaviour

D   Professional competence and due care

E   Integrity

32 TAX ADVICE

Your best friend has recently started up in business and really needs some tax advice. Because they know you are training to be an accountant they have automatically assumed you are the right person to give advice.

Which fundamental ethical principle prevents you from advising your best friend particularly regarding the fact that it is tax advice that he is seeking?

A Confidentiality

B Objectivity

C Professional Behaviour

D Professional competence and due care

E Integrity

33 CLIENT DISCUSSION

You and a work colleague decide to go out for dinner after work. Whilst in the restaurant you start to discuss a client and the issues which this client is currently facing. Unbeknown to you the CEO of their major supplier is sat at the next table and hears everything which you have discussed.

Which fundamental ethical principle prevents you and your colleague from discussing this in public?

A Confidentiality

B Objectivity

C Professional Behaviour

D Professional competence and due care

E Integrity

34 ACCOUNTING LEGISLATION

Your work colleague has decided not to comply with the relevant accounting legislation when preparing a client's account as they 'can't be bothered'.

Which TWO fundamental ethical principles is your colleague in breach of?

A Confidentiality

B Objectivity

C Professional Behaviour

D Professional competence and due care

E Integrity

35 FRAUD

You have recently discovered that your manager is committing fraud. Your manager suspects that you know, and have threatened you with termination of your contract if you decide to whistle blow him.

Which threat to fundamental principles are you faced with?

A   Self Interest

B   Self Review

C   Familiarity

D   Advocacy

E   Intimidation

36 NEW CLIENT

Your company has recently taken on a new client and you have been asked to prepare the monthly management accounts. As soon as you start work on the accounts you realise that it is your Auntie's Company.

Which threat to principles are you faced with?

A   Self Interest

B   Self Review

C   Familiarity

D   Advocacy

E   Intimidation

37 3 Ps

What do the 3 Ps relate to in terms of balancing economic, environment and social needs?

A   People, Planet, Product

B   Planet, Place, Product

C   Profit, People, Planet

D   Price, People, Product

E   Profit, Place, People

38   SUSTAINABLE

Kapfin is looking to become more sustainable and a manager believes that she has come up with a few amazing suggestions.

Which ONE of these suggestions relates to sustainability?

A   Encourage all staff and students to use their own cars to travel to and from Kaplan.

B   Ensure all lights and computers are left on in the evening to prevent break-ins.

C   Encourage all students and staff to throw paper in the normal waste bin.

D   Encourage all AAT Kaplan staff to work through their lunch.

E   To look into the possibility of providing the AAT textbook via e-books instead of providing a paper copy to students.

39   SUSTAINABILITY

Your friend is being encouraged to make a suggestion of how to improve sustainability within her workplace.

Which ONE of the following suggestions should she put forward to her manager?

A   Encourage all staff to print their work and maintain in lever arch files for audit trail purposes.

B   Look at installing motion sensor lights into the office block.

C   Encourage the Financial Accountant to replace his 2.0L Diesel BMW with a 3.5L Petrol BMW.

D   Suggest that all Monthly regional meetings should be done in the most central regional office.

E   Ensure all trainee accountants complete their CPD.

40   SOLAR PANELS

A company is trying to improve sustainability and it is considering installing solar panels on the office roof to reduce their yearly electricity costs. However the initial costs of implementing this is 20% higher than originally budgeted for.

From a sustainability perspective, should the company still pursue this even though it is going to have an adverse impact on cost?

A   Yes

B   No.

41 CSR OBJECTIVESS

Review each of the practical situations below, and match each situation with the appropriate corporate social responsibility (CSR) objective from the drop-down menu. You may use a CSR objective more than once if required.

Practical situation	CSR objective
Your organisation has a policy of encouraging all members of the finance department study for an appropriate accountancy qualification and proving financial support for those who do so.	
Your organisation will shortly introduce 'paperless office' procedures whereby all customer orders are processed online and an accounting software package maintains the sales and purchase ledger accounts.	
Your organisation issues a "Corporate Policy of Ethical Practices" which it requires all potential suppliers to agree to before purchasing goods and services from them	
Your organisation is currently installing lighting with movement sensors, so that lighting will automatically be switched off if no movement is sensed for 5 minutes. The lighting can be activated by movement only.	
Your organisation has a policy, wherever practicable, of permitting employees to work flexible hours, including working from home.	

Drop-down menu choices:

Environmentally-friendly policies   Ethical employment practices

Ethical business practices

42 BENEFITS

(a) **Identify TWO benefits to the community from the list below if an organisation introduces corporate social responsibility policies.**

   A   Employee absence from work

   B   Use of corporate resources to benefit the community

   C   Employees using voluntary days of absence from work to support charitable activities.

   D   Greater use of recycled materials

(b) **Identify TWO benefits to the environment from the list below if an organisation introduces corporate social responsibility policies.**

   A   Employee absence from work

   B   Greater use of renewable resources to reduce waste

   C   Employees using voluntary days of absence from work to support charitable activities.

   D   Greater use of recycled materials

43 CORPORATE SOCIAL RESPONSIBILITY

Which THREE of the following initiatives will minimise the environmental impact of an organisation's business activities?

- Ensuring company cars purchased have high CO2 emissions

- Offering free membership at a local gym

- Encouraging staff travel to work using public transport rather than using their cars

- Ensuring machines maximise energy consumption

- Installing energy saving production equipment

- Asking staff to leave their computers on overnight

- Installing motion sensor lights which turn off when rooms are empty

44 EMPLOYEE WELFARE

Which THREE of the following initiatives will improve the welfare of employees in an organisation?

- Introducing flexible working conditions for staff

- Ensuring all staff complete at least 8 hours overtime per week

- Offering all staff training and support to those who wish to gain further qualifications

- Opening the office at weekends to allow staff to work on Saturdays and Sundays

- Providing an onsite gym for all staff to use

- Offering bonuses to senior management staff only

45 CORPORATE SOCIAL RESPONSIBILITY STATEMENTS

Identify whether each of the following statements is true or false.

Statement	True/False
Implementing corporate social responsibility initiatives incurs costs without benefits to the organisation.	
An organisation can expect to receive both financial and non-financial benefits as a consequence of implementing corporate social responsibility initiatives.	
Introducing corporate social responsibility initiatives should enhance the reputation of an organisation.	
Corporate social responsibility policies may result in an organisation changing its production methods and/or changing its sources of materials supplies.	

Section 2

PRACTICE QUESTIONS

ASSESSMENT OBJECTIVE 2

46   HLB WHOLESALE

On 1 Feb Painting Supplies Ltd delivered the following goods to a credit customer, HLB Wholesale.

Painting Supplies Ltd	
19 Edmund St	
Newcastle, NE6 5DJ	

Delivery note No. 46589
01 Feb 20XX

HLB Wholesale   **Customer account code:** HLB24
98 Back St
Consett
DH4 3PD

20 tins of white paint, product code SD19

The list price of the goods was £15 each plus VAT. HLB Wholesale are to be given a 10% trade discount and a 4% discount if they pay within 4 working days.

(a)   Complete the invoice below.

Painting Supplies Ltd
19 Edmund St
Newcastle, NE6 5DJ
VAT Registration No. 402 2958 02

HLB Wholesale   **Customer account code:**
98 Back St
Consett
DH4 3PD
Date: 1 Feb 20XX   **Delivery note number:**
                                                 Invoice No: 298

Quantity	Product code	Total list price £	Net amount after discount £	VAT £	Gross £

Painting Supplies Ltd offer a discount of 10% if their customers buy from them.

(b) **What is the name of this type of discount?**

Picklist: bulk discount, prompt payment discount, trade discount

47 MASHED LTD

On 1 Aug Hickory House delivered the following goods to a credit customer, Mashed Ltd.

Hickory House **22 Nursery Road** **Keighley, BD22 7BD**
Delivery note No. 472 01 Aug 20XX
Mashed Ltd **Customer account code:** MA87 42 Moorside Court Ilkley Leeds, LS29 4PR
20 flower pots, product code P10

The list price of the goods was £5 per flower pot plus VAT. Mashed Ltd is to be given a 10% trade discount and a 4% early payment discount.

(a) **Complete the invoice below.**

Hickory House
22 Nursery Road
Keighley, BD22 7BD

VAT Registration No. 476 1397 02

Mashed Ltd **Customer account code:**
42 Moorside Court
Ilkley
Leeds, LS29 4PR **Delivery note number:**

Date: 1 Aug 20XX

Invoice No: 47

Quantity of pots	Product code	Total list price £	Net amount after discount £	VAT £	Gross £

Hickory House offers each customer a discount if they buy over a certain quantity of goods.

(b) **What is the name of this type of discount?**

Picklist: Bulk discount, prompt payment discount, trade discount

48 SDB

Sales invoices have been prepared and partially entered in the sales day-book, as shown below.

(a) **Complete the entries in the sales day-book by inserting the appropriate figures for each invoice.**

(b) **Total the last five columns of the sales day-book.**

Sales day-book

Date 20XX	Details	Invoice number	Total £	VAT £	Net £	Sales type 1 £	Sales type 2 £
31 Dec	Poonams	105	3,600				3,000
31 Dec	D. Taylor	106		1,280		6,400	
31 Dec	Smiths	107	3,840		3,200		3,200
	Totals						

49 WILLIAM & SAMMY LTD

The account shown below is in the sales ledger of Hickory House. A cheque for £668 has now been received from this customer.

William and Sammy Ltd

Date 20XX	Details	Amount £	Date 20XX	Details	Amount £
1 June	Balance b/f	4,250	2 June	Bank	4,250
23 June	Sales invoice 255	1,876	15 June	Sales returns credit note 98	1,208
30 June	Sales Invoice 286	2,459			

(a) **Which item has not been included in the payment?**

Picklist: Balance b/f, Sales invoice 255, Sales invoice 286, Bank, Sales returns credit note 98

An invoice is being prepared to be sent to William and Sammy Ltd for £3,890 plus VAT of £778. A prompt payment discount of 4% will be offered for payment within 10 days.

(b) **What is the amount Hickory House should receive if payment is made within 10 days?**

£

(c) **What is the amount Hickory House should receive if payment is NOT made within 10 days?**

£

50 PIXIE PAPERS

A supply of paper has been delivered to Alpha Ltd by Pixie Paper. The purchase order sent from Alpha Ltd, and the invoice from Pixie Paper, are shown below.

Alpha Ltd

121 Baker St

Newcastle, NE1 7DJ

Purchase Order No. PO1792

To: Pixie Paper

Date: 5 Aug 20XX

Please supply 50 boxes of A4 paper product code 16257

Purchase price: £10 per box, plus VAT

Discount: less 10% trade discount, as agreed.

Pixie Paper

24 Eden Terrace, Durham, DH9 7TE

VAT Registration No. 464 392 401

Invoice No. 1679

Alpha Ltd
121 Baker St
Newcastle, NE1 7DJ
9 Aug 20XX

50 boxes of A4 paper, product code 16257 @ £10 each	£500
VAT	£100
Total	£600

Terms: 30 days net

Check the invoice against the purchase order and answer the following questions.

Has the correct product been supplied by Pixie Paper?	Y	N
Has the correct net price been calculated?	Y	N
Has the total invoice price been calculated correctly?	Y	N
What would be the VAT amount charged if the invoice was correct?	£_____	
What would be the total amount charged if the invoice was correct?	£_____	

51   FREDDIE LTD

Purchase invoices have been received and partially entered in the purchases day-book of Freddie Ltd, as shown below.

(a)   **Complete the first two entries in the purchases day-book by inserting the appropriate figures for each invoice.**

(b)   **Complete the final entry in the purchases day book by inserting the appropriate figures from the following invoice.**

Novot & Co

5 Pheasant Way, Essex, ES9 8BN

VAT Registration No. 453 098 541

Invoice No. 2176

Freddie Ltd

9 Banbury Street

Sheffield

31 July 20XX

10 boxes of product code 14212 @ £400 each	£4,000
VAT	£800
Total	£4,800
Payment terms 30 days	

Purchases day-book

Date 20XX	Details	Invoice number	Total £	VAT £	Net £	Product 14211 £	Product 14212 £
31 July	Box Ltd	2177			800	800	
31 July	Shrew Ltd	2175		2,400		12,000	
31 July	Novot & Co	2176					
	Totals						

52 HOLLY LTD

The account shown below is in the purchase ledger of AD Wholesale. A cheque for £4,770 has now been paid to this supplier.

Holly Ltd

Date 20XX	Details	Amount £	Date 20XX	Details	Amount £
			5 Jan	Balance b/f	1,500
15 Jan	Purchase return 251	540	19 Jan	Purchase invoice 3658	2,360
31 Jan	Purchase return 286	360	27 Jan	Purchase invoice 2987	1,450

(a) **Which item has been not been included in the payment, causing it to be overstated?**

```
[                                    ]
```

Picklist: Balance b/f, Purchase invoice 3658, Bank, Purchase returns 286, Purchase invoice 2987

An invoice has been received from Rickman Repairs for £860 plus VAT of £172. A prompt payment discount of 10% will be offered for payment within 30 days.

(b) **What is the amount we should pay, if we meet the 30 days requirement?**

```
£ [                                 ]
```

(c) **How much VAT is payable if the payment is NOT made in 30 days?**

```
£ [                                 ]
```

(d) **What is the amount we should pay if payment is NOT made within 30 days?**

```
£ [                                 ]
```

53   EP MANUFACTURERS

Shown below is a statement of account received from a credit supplier, and the supplier's account as shown in the purchases ledger of EP Manufacturers.

KLP Ltd

19 Mussell Street, Newcastle, NE4 8JH

To: EP Manufacturers
19 Edmund St
Newcastle, NE6 5DJ

STATEMENT OF ACCOUNT

Date 20XX	Invoice number	Details	Invoice amount £	Cheque amount £	Balance £
1 Jan	468	Goods	5,200		5,200
3 Jan	458	Goods	3,600		8,800
8 Jan		Cheque		1,400	7,400
19 Jan	478	Goods	800		8,200
21 Jan		Cheque		6,500	1,700
28 Jan	488	Goods	4,350		6,050

KLP Ltd

Date 20XX	Details	Amount £	Date 20XX	Details	Amount £
8 Jan	Bank	1,400	1 Jan	Purchases	5,200
21 Jan	Bank	6,500	3 Jan	Purchases	3,600
31 Jan	Bank	1,200	19 Jan	Purchases	800

(a)   **Which item is missing from the statement of account from KLP Ltd?**

Picklist: cheque for £1,200, invoice 468, Invoice 478, Cheque for £6,500, Invoice 488, Cheque for £1,400

(b)   **Which item is missing from the supplier account in EP Manufacturers' purchases ledger?**

Picklist: Invoice 468, Invoice 472, Invoice 478, Invoice 488, Purchase return £900, Cheque for £2,500

(c)   **Once the omitted items have been recorded, what is the agreed balance outstanding between EP Manufacturers and KLP Ltd?**

£

54   STANNY LTD

Ringo's Rings sends out cheques to suppliers on the last day of the month following the month of invoice. Below is an extract from the purchases ledger of Ringo's Rings.

Stanny Ltd

Date 20XX	Details	Amount £	Date 20XX	Details	Amount £
13 Feb	Purchases returns credit note 198	650	1 Feb	Balance b/f	4,650
19 Feb	Purchase return credit note 154	1,250	10 Feb	Purchases Invoice 694	2,300
28 Feb	Bank	4,650	11 Feb	Purchase invoice 658	3,640

(a) Complete the remittance advice note below.

> **Ringo Rings**
>
> **37 Parker Lane**
>
> **Stoke SK1 0KE**
>
> **REMITTANCE ADVICE**
>
> **To:** Stanny Ltd   **Date:** 31 Mar 20XX
>
> Please find attached our cheque in payment of the following amounts.
>
> | Invoice number | Credit note number | Amount £ |
> |---|---|---|
> | | | |
> | | | |
> | | | |
> | | | |
> | | | |
> | **Total amount paid** | | |

(b) Are these two statements true or false?

A remittance note is for ours and the supplier's records   T   F

A remittance note is sent by a supplier confirming amounts received from them   T   F

55 TOYWORLD

Shown below is a statement of account received from a credit supplier, and the supplier's account as shown in the purchases ledger of Hickory House

Toyworld

18 Landview Road

Skipton

BD27 4TU

To: Hickory House

22 Nursery Road

Keighley, BD22 7BD

STATEMENT OF ACCOUNT

Date 20XX	Invoice number	Details	Invoice amount £	Cheque amount £	Balance £
1 Jan	207	Goods	2,500		2,500
8 April	310	Goods	900		3,400
9 June		Cheque		3,400	0
17 Aug	504	Goods	500		500
18 Aug	505	Goods	4,000		4,500

Toyworld

Date 20XX	Details	Amount £	Date 20XX	Details	Amount £
9 June	Bank	3,400	1 Jan	Purchases	2,500
25 June	Bank	500	8 April	Purchases	900
			17 Aug	Purchases	500

(a) **Which item is missing from the statement of account from Toyworld?**

Picklist: Invoice 207, Invoice 310, Invoice 504, Invoice 505, Cheque for £3,400, Cheque for £500

(b) **Which item is missing from the supplier account in Hickory Houses' purchases ledger?**

Picklist: Invoice 207, Invoice 310, Invoice 504, Invoice 505, Cheque for £3,400, Cheque for £500

(c) **Assuming any differences between the statement of account from Toyworld and the supplier account in Hickory Houses' purchases ledger are simply due to omission errors, what is the amount owing to Toyworld?**

£ [   ]

56   GREY GARAGES

Grey Garages makes payments to suppliers by BACS on the 25th of every month and includes all items that have been outstanding for more than 10 days.

Below is a pre-printed remittance advice slip taken from a statement of account received from a supplier, Mulberry Motors, showing all items outstanding.

Complete the remittance advice ready for the next payment to Mulberry Motors.

Remittance advice			
To: Mulberry Motors			
From: Grey Garages			
Payment method:		**Date of payment:**	
Items outstanding			Tick if included in payment
Date 20XX	Details	Amount £	
23-Jun	Invoice 213	740	
06-Jul	Credit note 14	120	
13-Jul	Invoice 216	620	
19-Jul	Invoice 257	870	
Total amount paid		£	

57   ERRICO

The two invoices below were received on 5 June from credit suppliers who offer prompt payment discounts.

Invoices:

Giacomo
VAT registration 446 1552 01
Invoice number 1923

To: Errico	4 June 20XX
	£
4 product code 45 @ £14.50 each	58.00
VAT @ 20%	11.60
	————
Total	69.60

Terms: 3% prompt payment discount if payment is received within 7 days of the invoice date.

Gaetani
VAT registration 446 4742 01
Invoice number 4578

To: Errico	4 June 20XX
	£
3 product code 42a @ £11.50 each	34.50
VAT @ 20%	6.90
	————
Total	41.40

Terms: 5% prompt payment discount if payment is received within 5 days of the invoice date.

Calculate the amount to be paid to each supplier if the prompt payment discount is taken and show the date by which the supplier should receive the payment.

Supplier	£	Date by which the payment should be received by the supplier
Giacomo		
Gaetani		

58   LADY LTD

Given below is the purchases day book for Lady Ltd

Date	Invoice No.	Code	Supplier	Total	VAT	Net
1 Dec	03582	PL210	M Brown	300.00	50.00	250.00
5 Dec	03617	PL219	H Madden	183.55	30.59	152.96
7 Dec	03622	PL227	L Singh	132.60	22.10	110.50
10 Dec	03623	PL228	A Stevens	90.00	15.00	75.00
18 Dec	03712	PL301	N Shema	197.08	32.84	164.24
			Totals	**903.23**	**150.53**	**752.70**

You are required to:

- Post the totals of the purchases day book to the general ledger accounts given
- Post the invoices to the payables' accounts in the subsidiary ledger given.

General ledger

Purchases ledger control account

	£		£
		1 Dec Balance b/d	5,103.90

VAT account

	£		£
		1 Dec Balance b/d	526.90

Purchases account

	£		£
1 Dec balance b/d	22,379.52		

Subsidiary ledger

M Brown

	£		£
		1 Dec Balance b/d	68.50

H Madden

	£		£
		1 Dec Balance b/d	286.97

L Singh

	£		£
		1 Dec Balance b/d	125.89

A Stevens

	£		£
		1 Dec Balance b/d	12.36

N Shema

	£		£
		1 Dec Balance b/d	168.70

59 SPARKY LTD

The following credit transactions all took place on 31 July and have been entered into the sales returns day-book of Sparky Ltd as shown below. No entries have yet been made in the ledgers.

Sales returns day-book

Date 20XX	Details	Credit note number	Total £	VAT £	Net £
31 July	Clarkson Ltd	150C	1,680	280	1,400
31 July	Kyle & Co	151C	720	120	600
	Totals		2,400	400	2,000

(a) **What will be the entries in the sales ledger?**

Sales ledger

Account name	Amount £	Debit ✓	Credit ✓

Picklist: Net, Purchases, Purchases ledger control, Clarkson Ltd, Purchases returns, Sales, Sales ledger control, Sales returns, Kyle & Co, Total, VAT

(b) **What will be the entries in the general ledger?**

General ledger

Account name	Amount £	Debit ✓	Credit ✓

Picklist: Kyle & Co, Net, Purchases, Purchases ledger control, Purchases returns, Sales, Sales ledger control, Sales returns, Clarkson Ltd, Total, VAT

60 LOUIS LTD

The following transactions all took place on 31 Jan and have been entered into the sales day book of Louis Ltd as shown below. No entries have yet been made into the ledger system.

Date 20XX	Details	Invoice number	Total £	VAT £	Net £
31 Jan	Sheep & Co	1400	3,840	640	3,200
31 Jan	Cow Ltd	1401	11,760	1,960	9,800
31 Jan	Chicken & Partners	1402	6,720	1,120	5,600
31 Jan	Pig Ltd	1403	14,496	2,416	12,080
	Totals		36,816	6,136	30,680

(a) **What will be the entries in the sales ledger?**

Account name	Amount £	Debit ✓	Credit ✓

Picklist: Sheep & Co, Purchases, Sales ledger control, Cow Ltd, Purchases returns, Sales, Chicken & Partners, Purchases ledger control, Sales returns, VAT, Pig Ltd

(b) **What will be the entries in the general ledger?**

Account name	Amount £	Debit ✓	Credit ✓

Picklist: Purchases ledger control, Sales, Sales ledger control, Purchases, VAT

61   THOMAS & TILLY

The following credit transactions all took place on 31 Jan and have been entered into the purchase returns day-book of Thomas & Tilly as shown below. No entries have yet been made in the ledgers.

Purchase returns day-book

Date 20XX	Details	Credit note number	Total £	VAT £	Net £
31 Jan	May Ltd	230C	1,920	320	1,600
31 Jan	Hammond & Co	231C	1,200	200	1,000
	Totals		3,120	520	2,600

(a)   **What will be the entries in the purchases ledger?**

Purchase ledger

Account name	Amount £	Debit ✓	Credit ✓

Picklist: Net, Purchases, Purchases ledger control, May Ltd, Purchases returns, Sales, Sales ledger control, Sales returns, VAT, Hammond & Co, Total.

(b)   **What will be the entries in the general ledger?**

General ledger

Account name	Amount £	Debit ✓	Credit ✓

Picklist: May Ltd, Net, Purchases, Purchases ledger control, Purchases returns, Sales, Sales ledger control, Sales returns, Hammond & Co, Total, VAT

62   JESSICA & CO

The following credit transactions all took place on 31 Dec and have been entered into the purchases returns day-book as shown below. No entries have yet been made in the ledgers.

Purchases returns day-book

Date 20XX	Details	Credit note number	Total £	VAT £	Net £
31 Dec	Iona Ltd	4763	1,680	280	1,400
31 Dec	Matilda Ltd	2164	4,320	720	3,600
	Totals		6,000	1,000	5,000

(a) **What will be the entries in the purchases ledger?**

Purchases ledger

Account name	Amount £	Debit ✓	Credit ✓

Picklist: Iona Ltd, Matilda Ltd, Net, Purchases, Purchases ledger control, Purchases returns, Sales, Sales ledger control, Sales returns, Total, VAT

(b) **What will be the entries in the general ledger?**

General ledger

Account name	Amount £	Debit ✓	Credit ✓

Picklist: Iona Ltd, Matilda Ltd, Net, Purchases, Purchases ledger control, Purchases returns, Sales, Sales ledger control, Sales returns, VAT, Total

63 HORSEY REACH

The following transactions all took place on 31 July and have been entered into the discounts allowed day book of Horsey Reach as shown below. No entries have yet been made into the ledger system.

Date 20XX	Details	Credit note number	Total £	VAT £	Net £
31 July	Ashleigh Buildings	145	36.00	6.00	30.00
31 July	143 WGT	146	54.00	9.00	45.00
31 July	McDuff McGregor	147	43.20	7.20	36.00
31 July	Cameron Travel	148	93.60	15.60	78.00
	Totals		226.80	37.80	189.00

(a) **What will be the entries in the general ledger?**

Account name	Amount £	Debit ✓	Credit ✓

Picklist: 13 WGT, Ashleigh Buildings, Cameron Travel, Discounts Allowed, Discounts Received, McDuff McGregor, Purchases, Purchases ledger control, Sales, Sales ledger control, VAT

(b) **What will be the entries in the subsidiary ledger?**

Account name	Amount £	Debit ✓	Credit ✓

Picklist: 143 WGT, Ashleigh Buildings, Cameron Travel, Discounts Allowed, Discounts Received, McDuff McGregor, Purchases, Purchases ledger control, Sales, Sales ledger control, VAT

64 BUTTERFLY BEES

These are the totals from the discounts received book of Butterfly Bees at the end of the month.

Total £	VAT £	Net £
427.20	71.20	356.00

(a) **What will be the entries in the general ledger?**

Account name	Amount £	Debit ✓	Credit ✓

One of the entries in the discounts received day book is for a credit note received from Bella Bumps for £20 plus VAT.

(b) **What will be the entry in the purchases ledger?**

Account name	Amount £	Debit ✓	Credit ✓

65   OLIVIA ROSE BRIDAL SUPPLIES

These are the totals from the discounts allowed book of Olivia Rose Bridal Supplies at the end of the month.

Total £	VAT £	Net £
226.80	37.80	189.00

(a)   What will be the entries in the general ledger?

Account name	Amount £	Debit ✓	Credit ✓

One of the entries in the discounts allowed day book is for a credit note sent to Bridezilla for £45 plus VAT.

(b)   What will be the entry in the sales ledger?

Account name	Amount £	Debit ✓	Credit ✓

66   CHUGGER LTD

The following transactions all took place on 31 July and have been entered in the credit side of the cash-book as shown below. No entries have yet been made in the ledgers.

Cash-book – Credit side

Date 20XX	Details	VAT £	Bank £
31 July	Stationery	16	96
31 July	Photocopier repair	40	240

(a)   What will be the entries in the general ledger?

General ledger

Account name	Amount £	Debit ✓	Credit ✓

Picklist: Stationery, Insurance, Repairs, Purchases ledger control, Sales ledger control, VAT

The following transactions all took place on 31 July and have been entered in the debit side of the cash-book as shown below. No entries have yet been made in the ledgers.

Cash-book – Debit side

Date 20XX	Details	Bank £
31 July	Balance b/f	6,350
31 July	BBG Ltd	7,200
31 July	EFG Ltd	5,000

(b) **What will be the TWO entries in the sales ledger?**

Sales ledger

Account name	Amount £	Debit ✓	Credit ✓

Picklist: Balance b/f, Sales ledger control, BBG Ltd, Purchases ledger control, EFG Ltd, Bank

(c) **What will be the entry in the general ledger?**

General ledger

Account name	Amount £	Debit ✓	Credit ✓

Picklist: Balance b/f, EFG Ltd Purchase ledger control, Sales ledger control, VAT, Bank, BBG Ltd

67 ITALIAN STALLIONS

The following transactions all took place on 31 Jan and have been entered in the credit side of the cash-book of Italian Stallions Ltd as shown below. No entries have yet been made in the ledgers.

Cash-book – Credit side

Date 20XX	Details	VAT £	Bank £
31 Jan	Printer repair	32	192
31 Jan	Paper	16	96

(a)   **What will be the entries in the general ledger?**

General ledger

Account name	Amount £	Debit ✓	Credit ✓

Picklist: Repairs, Office supplies, Purchases ledger control, Sales ledger control, VAT

The following transactions all took place on 31 Jan and have been entered in the debit side of the cash-book as shown below. No entries have yet been made in the ledgers.

Cash-book – Debit side

Date 20XX	Details	Bank £
31 Jan	Balance b/f	5,100
31 Jan	AAG Ltd	4,000
31 Jan	HLG Ltd	3,000

(b)   **What will be the TWO entries in the sales ledger?**

Sales ledger

Account name	Amount £	Debit ✓	Credit ✓

Picklist: Balance b/f, Sales ledger control, AAG Ltd, Purchases ledger control, HLG Ltd, Bank

(c)   **What will be the entry in the general ledger?**

General ledger

Account name	Amount £	Debit ✓	Credit ✓

Picklist: Balance b/f, EFG Ltd Purchase ledger control, Sales ledger control, VAT, Bank, BBG Ltd

68   FRED'S FISH

The following transactions all took place on 31 Dec and have been entered in the debit side of the cash-book as shown below. No entries have yet been made in the ledgers.

Cash-book – Debit side

Date 20XX	Details	Bank £
31 Dec	Balance b/f	4,280
31 Dec	K and D Ltd	8,200

(a)   **What will be the entry in the sales ledger?**

Sales ledger

Account name	Amount £	Debit ✓	Credit ✓

Picklist: Balance b/f, Bank, Purchases ledger control, K and D Ltd, Sales ledger control

(b)   **What will be the entry in the general ledger?**

General ledger

Account name	Amount £	Debit ✓	Credit ✓

Picklist: Balance b/f, Bank, Purchases ledger control, K and D Ltd, Sales ledger control

The following transactions all took place on 31 Dec and have been entered in the credit side of the cash-book as shown below. No entries have yet been made in the ledgers.

Cash-book – Credit side

Date 20XX	Details	VAT £	Bank £
31 Dec	Stationery	20	120
31 Dec	Postage		800

(c)   **What will be the entries in the general ledger?**

General ledger

Account name	Amount £	Debit ✓	Credit ✓

Picklist: Bank, Postage, Stationery, Purchases ledger control, Sales ledger control, VAT

69   ABC LTD

There are five payments to be entered in ABC Ltd's cash book.

Receipts

Received cash with thanks for goods bought.	Received cash with thanks for goods bought.	Received cash with thanks for goods bought.
From ABC Ltd, a customer without a credit account.	From ABC Ltd, a customer without a credit account.	From ABC Ltd, a customer without a credit account.
Net £180 VAT £36 Total £216	Net £220 VAT £44 Total £264	Net £530 (No VAT)
S. Lampard	*S Bobbins*	*Penny Rhodes*

Cheque book counterfoils

Henley's Ltd (Purchase ledger account HEN002) £4,925 000372	Epic Equipment Maintenance (We have no credit account with this supplier) £480 (incl VAT at 20%) 000373

(a)   **Enter the details from the three receipts and two cheque book stubs into the credit side of the cash-book shown below and total each column.**

Cash-book – credit side

Details	Cash	Bank	VAT	Payables	Cash purchases	Repairs and renewals
Balance b/f						
S. Lampard						
S. Bobbins						
Penny Rhodes						
Henley's Ltd						
Epic Equipment Maintenance						
Total						

There are two cheques from credit customers to be entered in ABC Ltd's cash book:

D. Davies   £851

E. Denholm £450

(b) **Enter the above details into the debit side of the cash-book and total each column.**

Cash book – debit side

Details	Cash	Bank	Receivables
Balance b/f	1,550	7,425	
D Davies			
E Denholm			
Total			

(c) **Using your answers to (a) and (b) above calculate the cash balance.**

£

(d) **Using your answers to (a) and (b) above calculate the bank balance.**

£

(e) **Will the bank balance brought down calculated in (d) above be a debit or credit balance?**

Debit/Credit

70 BEDS

There are five transactions to be entered in Beds' cash book.

Receipts

Received cash with thanks for goods bought.	Received cash with thanks for goods bought.	Received cash with thanks for goods bought.
From Beds, a customer without a credit account.	From Beds, a customer without a credit account.	From Beds, a customer without a credit account.
Net £590	Net £190	Net £230
VAT £118	VAT £38	(No VAT)
Total £708	Total £228	
A. Blighty Ltd	*R Bromby*	*Roxy Bland*

Cheque book counterfoils

Burgess Ltd	Fast Equipment Repairs
(Purchase ledger account BUR003)	(We have no credit account with this supplier)
£2,400	£96 (inc VAT at 20%)
No. 000101	No. 000102

(a) Enter the details from the three receipts and two cheque book stubs into the credit side of the cash-book shown below and total each column.

Cash-book – credit side

Details	Cash	Bank	VAT	Payables	Cash purchases	Repairs and renewals
Balance b/f						
A. Blighty Ltd						
R Bromby						
Roxy Bland						
Burgess Ltd						
Fast Equipment Repairs						
Total						

There are two cheques from credit customers to be entered in Beds' cash book:

A. Barnett   £698

H. Connelly   £250

(b) Enter the above details into the debit side of the cash-book and total each column.

Cash book – debit side

Details	Cash	Bank	Receivables
Balance b/f	1,175	3,825	
A Barnett			
H Connelly			
Total			

(c) Using your answers to (a) and (b) above calculate the cash balance.

£

(d) Using your answers to (a) and (b) above calculate the bank balance.

£

(e) Will the bank balance brought down calculated in (d) above be a debit or credit balance?

Debit/Credit

71   HICKORY HOUSE

Hickory House maintains a petty cash book as both a book of prime entry and part of the double entry accounting system. The following transactions all took place on 31 Dec and have been entered in the petty cash-book as shown below. No entries have yet been made in the general ledger.

Petty cash-book

Date 20XX	Details	Amount £	Date 20XX	Details	Amount £	VAT £	Postage £	Motor expenses £	Office expenses
31 Dec	Balance b/f	210.00	31 Dec	Stapler	6.72	1.12			5.60
31 Dec	Bank	90.00	31 Dec	Stamps	15.00		15.00		
			31 Dec	Parking	14.88	2.48		12.40	
			31 Dec	Stationery	19.20	3.20			16.00
			31 Dec	Balance c/d	244.20				
		300.00			300.00	6.80	15.00	12.40	21.60

What will be the FIVE entries in the general ledger?

General ledger

Account name	Amount £	Debit ✓	Credit ✓

Picklist: Balance b/f, Balance c/d, Bank, Stationery, Stapler, Motor expenses, Parking, Office expenses, Petty cash-book, Stamps, Postage, VAT

72   MESSI & CO

Messi & Co maintains a petty cash book as a book of prime entry; it is not part of the double entry accounting system. The following transactions all took place on 31 Dec and have been entered in the petty cash-book as shown below. No entries have yet been made in the general ledger.

Petty cash-book

Date 20XX	Details	Amount £	Date 20XX	Details £	Amount £	VAT £	Postage £	Motor expenses £	Office expenses £
31 Dec	Op balance	100.00	31 Dec	Paper	27.33	4.55			22.78
			31 Dec	Stamps	4.50		4.50		
			31 Dec	Biscuits	6.60	1.10			5.50
			31 Dec	Parking	9.60	1.60		8.00	
			31 Dec	Cl balance	51.97				
		100.00			100.00	7.25	4.50	8.00	28.28

What will be the FIVE entries in the general ledger?

General ledger

Account name	Amount £	Debit ✓	Credit ✓

Picklist: Balance b/f, Balance c/d, Bank, Motor expenses, Paper, Parking, Petty cash control, Office expenses, Petty cash-book, Stamps, Postage, VAT

73 YUMMY CUPCAKES

Yummy Cupcakes maintains a petty cash book as a book of prime entry; it is not part of the double entry accounting system. The following transactions all took place on 31 July and have been entered in the petty cash-book as shown below. No entries have yet been made in the general ledger.

Petty cash-book

Date 20XX	Details	Amount £	Date 20XX	Details £	Amount £	VAT £	Sundry expenses £	Business travel £	Postage
1 July	Op balance	150.00	31 July	Parking	15.00	2.50		12.50	
			31 July	Tea & Coffee	12.00	2.00	10.00		
			31 July	Travel	39.44	6.57		32.87	
			31 July	Stamps	4.00				4.00
			31 July	Cl balance	79.56				
		150.00			150.00	11.07	10.00	45.37	4.00

What will be the FIVE entries in the general ledger?

General ledger

Account name	Amount £	Debit ✓	Credit ✓

Picklist: Postage, Balance c/d, Bank, Fuel, Balance b/f, Motor repair, Sundry expenses, Petty cash-book, VAT, Business Travel

74   BROOKLYN BOATS

The following two accounts are in the general ledger of Brooklyn Boats at the close of day on 31 Dec.

(a)   Insert the balance carried down together with date and details.

(b)   Insert the totals.

(c)   Insert the balance brought down together with date and details.

Electricity

Date 20XX	Details	Amount £	Date 20XX	Details £	Amount £
01 Dec	Balance b/f	870			
12 Dec	Bank	350			
	Total			Total	

Picklist: Balance b/d, Balance c/d, Bank, Closing balance, Opening balance, Purchases ledger control

Discounts received

Date 20XX	Details	Amount £	Date 20XX	Details £	Amount £
			1 Dec	Bal b/f	500
			15 Dec	Purchase ledger control	100
	Total			Total	

Picklist: Balance b/d, Balance c/d, Bank, Closing balance, Opening balance, Sales ledger control

75   CRAZY CURTAINS

The following two accounts are in the general ledger of Crazy Curtains at the close of day on 31 Jan.

(a)   **Insert the balance carried down together with date and details.**

(b)   **Insert the totals.**

(c)   **Insert the balance brought down together with date and details.**

Electricity expense

Date 20XX	Details	Amount £	Date 20XX	Details £	Amount £
01 Jan	Bal b/f	200			
22 Jan	Bank	250			
	Total			**Total**	

Picklist: Balance b/d, Balance c/d, Bank, Closing balance, Opening balance, Electricity Expense

Rental income

Date 20XX	Details	Amount £	Date 20XX	Details £	Amount £
			01 Jan	Balance b/f	400
			28 Jan	Bank	600
	Total			**Total**	

Picklist: Balance b/d, Balance c/d, Bank, Closing balance, Opening balance, Sales ledger control

77   SMITH & SON

Below is a list of balances to be transferred to the trial balance of Smith & Son at 31 Dec.

Place the figures in the debit or credit column, as appropriate, and total each column.

Account name	Amount £	Debit £	Credit £
Fixtures and fittings	8,250		
Capital	18,400		
Bank overdraft	4,870		
Petty cash control	350		
Sales ledger control (SLCA)	42,870		
Purchases ledger control (PLCA)	23,865		
VAT owed to tax authorities	10,245		
Inventory	9,870		
Loan from bank	22,484		
Sales	180,264		
Sales returns	5,420		
Purchases	129,030		
Purchases returns	2,678		
Discount allowed	2,222		
Discount received	3,432		
Heat and Light	1,490		
Motor expenses	2,354		
Wages	42,709		
Rent and rates	10,600		
Repairs	3,020		
Hotel expenses	1,890		
Telephone	2,220		
Delivery costs	1,276		
Miscellaneous expenses	2,667		
Totals			

77 EXPIALIDOCIOUS LTD

Below is a list of balances to be transferred to the trial balance of Expialidocious Ltd as at 31 July.

Place the figures in the debit or credit column, as appropriate, and total each column.

Account name	Amount £	Debit £	Credit £
Capital	25,360		
Petty cash control	250		
Loan from bank	11,600		
Sales ledger control (SLCA)	159,242		
Purchases ledger control (PLCA)	83,682		
Motor vehicles	35,900		
Inventory	28,460		
Bank overdraft	10,063		
VAT owed from tax authorities	15,980		
Purchases	343,014		
Purchases returns	1,515		
Wages	56,150		
Motor expenses	2,950		
Interest income	400		
Sales	532,900		
Sales returns	5,760		
Stationery	1,900		
Light & heat	6,500		
Discount received	200		
Discount allowed	2,160		
Interest paid on overdraft	550		
Travel	1,800		
Marketing	650		
Telephone	1,510		
Miscellaneous expenses	2,944		
Totals			

Section 3

PRACTICE QUESTIONS

ASSESSMENT OBJECTIVE 3

78   INTREPID INTERIORS

(a)   Intrepid Interiors has started a new business, Intrepid Exteriors, and a new set of accounts are to be opened. A partially completed journal to record the opening entries is shown below.

Record the journal entries needed in the accounts in the general ledger of Intrepid Exteriors to deal with the opening entries.

Account name	Amount £	Debit ✓	Credit ✓
Cash at bank	7,250		
Bank loan	5,000		
Capital	10,625		
Motor vehicles	4,750		
Insurances	575		
Stationery	300		
Sundry expenses	225		
Motor expenses	135		
Advertising	990		
Rent and rates	1,400		
Journal to record the opening entries of new business			

(b)   **From the list below, select which one of the following transactions would be recorded in the journal.**

Picklist: Credit sale, contra, electricity expense, reimbursement of petty cash

79   DOWN & OUT

Down & Out pays it employees by cheque every month and maintains a wages control account. A summary of last month's payroll transactions is shown below:

Item	£
Gross wages	8,542
Employer's NI	1,025
Employees' NI	940
Income tax	1,708
Trade union fees	425

Record the journal entries needed in the general ledger to:

(i)   Record the wages expense

(ii)   Record the HM Revenue & Customs liability

(iii)   Record the net wages paid to the employees

(iv)   Record the trade union liability.

(i)

Account name	Amount £	Debit ✓	Credit ✓

(ii)

Account name	Amount £	Debit ✓	Credit ✓

(iii)

Account name	Amount £	Debit ✓	Credit ✓

(iv)

Account name	Amount £	Debit ✓	Credit ✓

Picklist for each: Bank, Employees NI, Employers NI, HM Revenue and Customs, Income Tax, Net wages, Trade union, Wages control, Wages expense.

80   RHYME TIME

Rhyme Time pays its employees by cheque every month and maintains a wages control account. A summary of last month's payroll transactions is shown below:

Item	£
Gross wages	10,130
Employers' NI	1,185
Employees' NI	1,006
Income tax	2,835
Employer's pension contributions	600
Employee's Pension contributions	550

Record the journal entries needed in the general ledger to:

(i)   Record the wages expense

(ii)   Record the HM Revenue and Customs liability

(iii)   Record the net wages paid to the employees

(iv)   Record the pension liability.

(i)

Account name	Amount £	Debit ✓	Credit ✓

(ii)

Account name	Amount £	Debit ✓	Credit ✓

(iii)

Account name	Amount £	Debit ✓	Credit ✓

(iv)

Account name	Amount £	Debit ✓	Credit ✓

81   BEDROOM BITS

A credit customer, ABC Ltd, has ceased trading, owing Bedroom Bits £2,400 including VAT.

Record the journal entries needed in the general ledger to write off the net amount and the VAT.

Account name	Amount £	Debit ✓	Credit ✓

Picklist: Irrecoverable debts, ABC Ltd, Bedroom Bits, Purchases, Purchases ledger control, Sales, Sales ledger control, VAT.

82   CHESTNUT

On 1 December, Chestnut had a balance of £46,000 on its SLCA and £31,000 on its PLCA. It also sold goods to Cook Ltd, one of its main suppliers for £4,000. Cook was owed £12,000 for goods it had sold to Chestnut.

Perform a contra and balance off the ledger accounts below. Dates are not required.

SLCA

Details	Amount £	Details	Amount £

PLCA

Details	Amount £	Details	Amount £

83   BEANZ

This is a customer's account in the sales ledger.

Beanz Co

Details	Amount £	Details	Amount £
Balance b/f	4,530	Payment received	2,100
Invoice SD4564	3,210	Credit note	420

The customer has now ceased trading.

Record the journal entries needed to write off the receivable, including VAT.

Account name	Amount £	Debit ✓	Credit ✓

Picklist: Irrecoverable debts, Beanz Co, Purchases, Purchases ledger control, Sales, Sales ledger control, VAT.

84   RENT ERROR

An entry to record a bank receipt of £500 for rent has been reversed.

Record the journal entries needed in the general ledger to:

(i)   remove the incorrect entry

(ii)   record the correct entry.

(i)

Account name	Amount £	Debit ✓	Credit ✓

(ii)

Account name	Amount £	Debit ✓	Credit ✓

Picklist for all above: Bank, Cash, Rent Received, Purchases, Purchases ledger control, Sales, Sales ledger control, Suspense, VAT.

85   GAS ERROR

An entry to record a gas expense of £300 was made correctly in the bank but was posted to electricity expenses instead of gas expenses.

Record the journal entries needed in the general ledger to record the correction.

Account name	Amount £	Debit ✓	Credit ✓

86   BUILDING ERROR

An entity purchased a new building for £400,000. This amount was debited to the buildings account, but £40,000 was credited to the bank account.

Record the journal entries needed in the general ledger to record the correction.

Account name	Amount £	Debit ✓	Credit ✓

87   SALES ERROR

A credit sale of £12,000 including VAT has been made. The full £12,000 has been debited to the SLCA and credited to sales.

Record the journal entries needed in the general ledger to record the correction.

Account name	Amount £	Debit ✓	Credit ✓

88   CB INTERIORS

CB Interiors' initial trial balance includes a suspense account with a balance of £8,640.

The error has been traced to the purchases day-book shown below.

Purchases day-book

DATE 20XX	Details	Invoice number	Total £	VAT £	Net £
30 Jun	Able Paints Ltd	2,763	2,400	400	2,000
30 Jun	Matley Materials	2,764	3,120	520	2,600
30 Jun	Teesdale Parts	2,765	4,080	680	3,400
	Totals		960	1,600	8,000

Identify the error and record the journal entries needed in the general ledger to

(i) **remove the incorrect entry**

(ii) **record the correct entry**

(iii) **remove the suspense account balance.**

(i)

Account name	Amount £	Debit ✓	Credit ✓

(ii)

Account name	Amount £	Debit ✓	Credit ✓

(iii)

Account name	Amount £	Debit ✓	Credit ✓

Picklist for all above: Able Paints Ltd, Matley Materials, Teesdale Parts, Purchases, Purchases day-book, Purchases ledger control, Purchases returns, Purchases returns day-book, Sales, Sales day-book, Sales ledger control, Sales returns, Sales returns day-book, Suspense, VAT.

89 ROGER DODGER

Roger Dodger's initial trial balance includes a suspense account with a balance of £360.

The error has been traced to the purchase returns day-book shown below.

Purchase returns day-book

Date 20XX	Details	Note number	Total £	VAT £	Net £
30 Jun	Dennis Designs Ltd	421	1,200	200	1,000
30 Jun	XYZ Ltd	422	1,920	320	1,600
30 Jun	Denby Prints	423	4,800	800	4,000
	Totals		7,920	1,680	6,600

Identify the error and record the journal entries needed in the general ledger to:

(i) **remove the incorrect entry**

(ii) **record the correct entry**

(iii) **remove the suspense account balance.**

(i)

Account name	Amount £	Debit ✓	Credit ✓

(ii)

Account name	Amount £	Debit ✓	Credit ✓

(iii)

Account name	Amount £	Debit ✓	Credit ✓

Picklist for all above: Dennis Designs Ltd, XYZ Ltd, Denby Prints, Purchases, Purchases day-book, Purchases ledger control, Purchases returns, Purchases returns day-book, Sales, Sales day-book, Sales ledger control, Sales returns, Sales returns day-book, Suspense, VAT.

90   BUCKLEY DRAINS

Buckley Drains' trial balance was extracted and did not balance. The debit column of the trial balance totalled £336,728 and the credit column totalled £325,923.

(a)   **What entry would be made in the suspense account to balance the trial balance?**

Account name	Amount £	Debit ✓	Credit ✓
Suspense			

(b)   The error has been traced to an unpaid invoice for advertising, which was recorded correctly in advertising expenses but nowhere else.

Record the journal entries needed in the general ledger to record the correction.

Account name	Amount £	Debit ✓	Credit ✓

(c)   **Show one reason for maintaining the journal**

	✓
To correct errors only	
To correct errors and record transactions that have not been recorded in any other book of prime entry	
To record transactions from every other book of prime entry.	

91   MENDONCA

Mendonca's trial balance was extracted and did not balance. The debit column of the trial balance totalled £643,475 and the credit column totalled £641,495

(a)   **What entry would be made in the suspense account to balance the trial balance?**

Account name	Amount £	Debit ✓	Credit ✓

(b)   The error has been traced to the posting of the wages payment. The total payment made was £3,200. This was incorrectly made in both the wages and bank account. The amount recorded in wages was £2,300, with a credit to the bank of £320 shown.

Record the journal entries needed in the general ledger to record the correction.

Account name	Amount £	Debit ✓	Credit ✓

92   BEASANT

Beasant's trial balance was extracted and did not balance. The debit column of the trial balance totalled £630,000 and the credit column totalled £615,000.

(a)   **What entry would be made in the suspense account to balance the trial balance?**

Account name	Amount £	Debit ✓	Credit ✓
Suspense			

(b)   The error has been traced to a late credit sale. The full amount of the sale (including VAT) was correctly recorded in the SLCA but no other entries were made.

Record the journal entries needed in the general ledger to record the correction.

Account name	Amount £	Debit ✓	Credit ✓

(c)   **Show one reason for maintaining the journal**

	✓
To detect fraud	
To record non-regular transactions	
To record goods sold on credit	

93   HEARN

On 30 June Hearn extracted an initial trial balance which did not balance, and a suspense account was opened. On 1 July the following errors were noted:

1   A rent payment of £430 had been correctly included in the bank, but included within rent expenses as £340.

2   An irrecoverable debt of £600 plus VAT had been credited correctly credited to the SLCA, but the only debit entry was £600 to irrecoverable debts.

Complete the journal to correct the errors, and re-draft the trial balance by placing figures into the debit or credit column. You re-drafted trial balance should take into account the journal entries you have made.

Journal entries

Account name	Debit £	Credit £

	Balances extracted on 30 June £	Balances at 1 July	
		Debit £	Credit £
Sales ledger control	34,560		
Purchases ledger control	21,420		
VAT owing to HM Revenue and Customs	3,412		
Capital	50,000		
Sales	201,327		
Sales returns	1,465		
Purchases	87,521		
Purchase returns	252		
Plant and equipment	15,200		
Motor expenses	4,310		
Office expenses	10,321		
Rent and rates	21,420		
Heat and light	8,920		
Wages	53,205		
Irrecoverable debt	1,450		
Office equipment	42,030		
Bank overdraft	4201		
Suspense account (debit balance)	210		
Totals			

94   RODMAN

On 30 June Rodman extracted an initial trial balance which did not balance, and a suspense account was opened. On 1 July the following errors were noted:

1   A VAT refund of £1,250 received from HMRC was recorded in the bank, but no other entry was made.

2   A wages payment of £4,300 was credited to both the bank and wages.

Complete the journal to correct the errors, and re-draft the trial balance by placing figures into the debit or credit column. You re-drafted trial balance should take into account the journal entries you have made.

Journal entries

Account name	Debit £	Credit £

	Balances extracted on 30 June £	Balances at 1 July	
		Debit £	Credit £
Sales ledger control	38,070		
Purchases ledger control	20,310		
VAT owed from HM Revenue and Customs	2,510		
Capital	70,000		
Sales	153,488		
Sales returns	2,135		
Purchases	63,261		
Purchase returns	542		
Plant and equipment	17,319		
Motor expenses	3,214		
Office expenses	6,421		
Rent and rates	17,414		
Heat and light	6,421		
Wages	45,532		
Irrecoverable debt	1,532		
Office equipment	35,313		
Bank overdraft	2,152		
Suspense account (debit balance)	7,350		
Totals			

95   LUXURY BATHROOMS

On 28 April Luxury Bathrooms received the following bank statement as at 24 April.

	SKB Bank plc				
	68 London Road, Reading, RG8 4RN				
To: Luxury Bathrooms	Account No: 55548921			24 April 20XX	
	Statement of Account				
Date	**Detail**	**Paid out**	**Paid in**	**Balance**	
20XX		**£**	**£**	**£**	
03 April	Balance b/d			17,845	C
03 April	Cheque 120045	8,850		8,995	C
04 April	Bank Giro Ricketts & Co		465	9,460	C
04 April	Cheque 120046	2,250		7,210	C
05 April	Cheque 120047	64		7,146	C
08 April	Cheque 120048	3,256		3,890	C
14 April	Direct debit AMB Ltd	2,265		1,625	C
14 April	Direct debit D Draper	2,950		1,325	D
14 April	Cheque 120050	655		1,980	D
22 April	Paid in at SKB bank		2,150	170	C
22 April	Bank charges	63		107	C
23 April	Overdraft fee	25		82	C
	D = Debit C = Credit				

The cash book as at 24 April is shown below.

Cash book

Date	Details	Bank	Date	Cheque	Details	Bank
01 April	Balance b/d	17,845	01 April	120045	R Sterling Ltd	8,850
19 April	Olsen & Lane	2,150	01 April	120046	Bert Cooper	2,250
22 April	Frith Ltd	685	01 April	120047	Hetko & Sons	64
22 April	Hodgetts & Co	282	02 April	120048	Barrett Ltd	3,256
			02 April	120049	K Plomer	542
			08 April	120050	I&E Brown	655
			08 April	120051	T Roberts	1,698
			14 April		AMB Ltd	2,265

Details column options: Balance b/d, balance c/d, Bank charges, R Sterling Ltd, Olsen & Lane, Frith Ltd, Hodgetts & Co, Bert Cooper, Hetko & Sons, Barrett Ltd, K Plomer, I&E Brown, T Roberts, AMB Ltd, Ricketts & Co, D Draper, Opening balance, Overdraft fees.

(a)   Check the items on the bank statement against the items in the cash book.

(b)   Enter any items in the cash book as needed.

(c)   Total the cash book and clearly show the balance carried down at 24 April (closing balance) and brought down at 25 April (opening balance).

96   WHOLESALE FLOORING

The bank statement and cash book for Wholesale Flooring is shown below.

Money Bags Bank PLC
52 Oak Road, Timperley, SK10 8LR

To: Wholesale Flooring   Account No: 47013799   23 June 20XX

Statement of Account

Date	Detail	Paid out	Paid in	Balance	
20XX		£	£	£	
04 June	Balance b/d			5,125	D
05 June	Cheque 104373	890		6,015	D
05 June	Cheque 104374	1,725		7,740	D
05 June	Cheque 104375	210		7,950	D
11 June	Cheque 104378	784		8,734	D
12 June	Bank Giro credit Aintree and Co		1,250	7,484	D
13 June	Cheque 104376	1,275		8,759	D
15 June	Cheque 104377	725		9,484	D
17 June	Paid in at Money Bags bank plc		550	8,934	D
20 June	Direct debit MD County council	400		9,334	D
23 June	Bank charges	160		9,494	D
23 June	Overdraft fee	90		9,584	D
	D = Debit C = Credit				

Cash book

Date 20XX	Details	Bank £	Date 20XX	Cheque number	Details	Bank £
			01 June		Balance b/d	5,125
16 June	Beeston's	550	01 June	104373	Good iron	890
19 June	Airfleet exteriors	3,025	01 June	104374	Ashworth & Co	1,725
22 June	Jones's	2,775	01 June	104375	Ironfit	210
			05 June	104376	OSS Ltd	1,275
			07 June	104377	Perfect tools	725
			08 June	104378	Campden Ltd	784
			14 June	104379	Thornley & Thwaite	675
			14 June	104380	Castle & Cove	178

Details columns options: Balance b/d, Balance c/d, Bank charges, Good Iron, Beeston's, Aintree & Co, Perfect Tools, Closing balance, Ashworth & Co, Thornley & Thwaite, MD County Council, Campden Ltd, Airfleet Exteriors, Castle & Cove, OSS Ltd, Opening balance, Overdraft Fee, Ironfit, Jones's.

(a)   Check the items on the bank statement against the items in the cash book.

(b)   Enter any items in the cash book as needed.

(c)   Total the cash book and clearly show the balance carried down at 23 June (closing balance) and brought down at 24 June (opening balance).

97   MCKEOWN

The bank statement and cash book for McKeown is shown below.

Money Bags Bank PLC

To: McKeown Ltd   Account No: 47013799   23 June 20XX

Statement of Account

Date 20XX	Detail	Paid out £	Paid in £	Balance £	
01 June	Balance b/d			7,420	C
01 June	Bank Giro credit Pond		180	7,600	C
01 June	Cheque 110156	420		7,180	C
01 June	Interest received		85	7,265	C
11 June	Cheque 110157	430		6,835	C
12 June	Cheque 110158	520		6,315	C
13 June	Cheque 110161	750		5,565	C
15 June	Bank Giro credit Sherwood		640	6,205	C
17 June	Paid in to Money Bags bank		1,200	7,405	C
20 June	Bank Giro credit Coyne		1,630	9,035	C
23 June	Direct debit Wilmott	300		8,735	C
23 June	Interest received		35	8,770	C

D = Debit   C = Credit

Cash book

Date 20XX	Details	Bank £	Date 20XX	Cheque number	Details	Bank £
01 June	Balance b/d	7,180	07 June	110157	Williams	430
12 June	Sherwood	640	07 June	110158	Forecast	520
14 June	Cash sales	1,200	07 June	110159	Beasant	1,240
22 June	Tweedy	860	07 June	110160	Davison	1,420
23 June	Butterwood	440	07 June	110161	Mildenhall	750

(a)   Check the items on the bank statement against the items in the cash book.

(b)   Enter any items in the cash book as needed.

(c)   Total the cash book and clearly show the balance carried down at 23 June (closing balance) and brought down at 24 June (opening balance).

98   LUXURY BATHROOMS

Below is the bank statement and updated cash book for Luxury Bathrooms.

SKB Bank plc					
68 London Road, Reading, RG8 4RN					
To: Luxury Bathrooms		Account No: 55548921		24 April 20XX	
Statement of Account					
Date	**Detail**		**Paid out**	**Paid in**	**Balance**
20XX			£	£	£
03 April	Balance b/d				17,845 C
03 April	Cheque 120045		8,850		8,995 C
04 April	Bank Giro Ricketts & Co			465	9,460 C
04 April	Cheque 120046		2,250		7,210 C
05 April	Cheque 120047		64		7,146 C
08 April	Cheque 120048		3,256		3,890 C
14 April	Direct debit AMB Ltd		2,265		1,625 C
14 April	Direct debit D Draper		2,950		1,325 D
14 April	Cheque 120050		655		1,980 D
22 April	Paid in at SKB Bank			2,150	170 C
22 April	Bank charges		63		107 C
23 April	Overdraft fee		25		82 C
D = Debit C = Credit					

Date	Details	Bank	Date	Cheque	Details	Bank
01 April	Balance b/d	17,845	01 April	120045	R Sterling Ltd	8,850
19 April	Olsen & Lane	2,150	01 April	120046	Bert Cooper	2,250
22 April	Frith Ltd	685	01 April	120047	Hetko & Sons	64
22 April	Hodgetts & Co	282	02 April	120048	Barrett Ltd	3,256
04 April	Ricketts & Co	465	02 April	120049	K Plomer	542
			08 April	120050	I&E Brown	655
			08 April	120051	T Roberts	1,698
			14 April		AMB Ltd	2,265
			14 April		D Draper	2,950
			22 April		Bank charges	63
			23 April		Overdraft fee	25
24 April	Balance c/d	1,191				
		22,618				**22,618**
			25 April		Balance b/d	1,191

Complete the bank reconciliation statement as at 24 April.

Note: Do not make any entries in the shaded boxes.

Bank reconciliation statement as at 24 April 20XX.

Balance per bank statement	£
Add:	
Name:	£
Name:	£
Total to add	£
Less:	
Name:	£
Name:	£
Total to subtract	£
Balance as per cash book	£

Name options: Bank charges, , R Sterling Ltd, Olsen & Lane, Frith Ltd, Hodgetts & Co, Bert Cooper, Hetko & Sons, Barrett Ltd, K Plomer, I&E Brown, T Roberts, AMB Ltd, Ricketts & Co, D Draper, Overdraft fees.

99 WHOLESALE FLOORING

Below is the bank statement and updated cash book for Wholesale Flooring.

	Money Bags Bank PLC **52 Oak Road, Timperley, SK10 8LR**				
To: Wholesale Flooring	Account No: 47013799		23 June 20XX		
	Statement of Account				
Date	**Detail**	**Paid out**	**Paid in**	**Balance**	
20XX		£	£	£	
04 June	Balance b/d			5,125	D
05 June	Cheque 104373	890		6,015	D
05 June	Cheque 104374	1,725		7,740	D
05 June	Cheque 104375	210		7,950	D
11 June	Cheque 104378	784		8,734	D
12 June	Bank Giro credit Aintree and Co		1,250	7,484	D
13 June	Cheque 104376	1,275		8,759	D
15 June	Cheque 104377	725		9,484	D
17 June	Paid in at Money Bags bank plc		550	8,934	D
20 June	Direct debit MD County council	400		9,334	D
23 June	Bank charges	160		9,494	D
23 June	Overdraft fee	90		9,584	D
	D = Debit C = Credit				

Date 20XX	Details	Bank £	Date 20XX	Cheque number	Details	Bank £
			01 June		Balance b/d	5,125
16 June	Beeston's	550	01 June	104373	Good Iron	890
19 June	Airfleet exteriors	3,025	01 June	104374	Ashworth & Co	1,725
22 June	Jones's	2,775	01 June	104375	Ironfit	210
12 June	Aintree & Co	1,250	05 June	104376	OSS Ltd	1,275
			07 June	104377	Perfect Tools	725
			08 June	104378	Campden Ltd	784
			14 June	104379	Thornley & Thwaite	675
			14 June	104380	Castle and Cove	178
			20 June		MD County council	400
			23 June		Bank charges	160
23 June	Balance c/d	4,637	23 June		Overdraft fee	90
		12,237				12,237
			24 June		Balance b/d	4,637

Complete the bank reconciliation statement as at 23 June.

Note: Do not make any entries in the shaded boxes.

Bank reconciliation statement as at 23 June 20XX

Balance per bank statement	£
Add:	
Name:	£
Name:	£
Total to add	£
Less:	
Name:	£
Name:	£
Total to subtract	£
Balance as per cash book	£

Name options: Bank charges, OSS Ltd, Beeston's, Aintree and Co, Ironfit, Campden Ltd, MD County Council, Ashworth & Co, Airfleet Exteriors, Thornley & Thwaite, Perfect Tools, Overdraft Fee, Castle & Cove, Good Iron, Jones's.

100 MCKEOWN

The bank statement and cash book for McKeown is shown below.

Money Bags Bank PLC

To: McKeown Ltd	Account No: 47013799	23 June 20XX

Statement of Account

Date	Detail	Paid out	Paid in	Balance	
20XX		£	£	£	
01 June	Balance b/d			7,420	C
01 June	Bank Giro credit Pond		180	7,600	C
01 June	Cheque 110156	420		7,180	C
01 June	Interest received		85	7,265	C
11 June	Cheque 110157	430		6,835	C
12 June	Cheque 110158	520		6,315	C
13 June	Cheque 110161	750		5,565	C
15 June	Bank Giro credit Sherwood		640	6,205	C
17 June	Paid in to Money Bags bank		1,200	7,405	C
20 June	Bank Giro credit Coyne		1,630	9,035	C
23 June	Direct debit Wilmott	300		8,735	C
23 June	Interest received		35	8,770	C
	D = Debit C = Credit				

Cash book

Date 20XX	Details	Bank £	Date 20XX	Cheque number	Details	Bank £
01 June	Balance b/d	7,180	07 June	110157	Williams	430
12 June	Sherwood	640	07 June	110158	Forecast	520
14 June	Cash sales	1,200	07 June	110159	Beasant	1,240
22 June	Tweedy	860	07 June	110160	Davison	1,420
23 June	Butterwood	440	07 June	110161	Mildenhall	750
01 June	Interest received	85	23 June		Wilmott	300
20 June	Coyne	1,630				
23 June	Interest received	35				

(a) Complete the bank reconciliation statement as at 23 June.

Note: Do not make any entries in the shaded boxes.

Bank reconciliation statement as at 23 June 20XX

Balance per bank statement	
Add:	
Name:	
Name:	
Total to add	
Less:	
Name:	
Name:	
Total to subtract	
Balance as per cash book	

(b) Refer to the cash book in (a) and check that the bank statement has correctly been reconciled by calculating:

– the balance carried down

– the total of each of the bank columns after the balance carried down has been recorded.

Balance carried down £	Bank column totals £

101 MONSTER MUNCHIES

This is a summary of transactions with customers of Monster Munchies during the month of June.

(a) Show whether each entry will be a debit or credit in the Sales ledger control account in the General ledger.

Details	Amount £	Debit ✓	Credit ✓
Balance of receivables at 1 June	48,000		
Goods sold on credit	12,415		
Receipts from credit customers	22,513		
Discount allowed	465		
Sales returns from credit customers	320		

(b) **What will be the balance brought down on 1 July on the above account?**

✓

Dr £37,117	
Cr £37,117	
Dr £83,713	
Cr £83,713	
Dr £58,883	
Cr £58,883	

The following debit balances were in the subsidiary (sales) ledger on 1 July.

	£
XXX Ltd	21,300
Brittle Homes Ltd	5,376
Colin and Campbell	333
Bashford Incorporated	1,733
Mainstreet Homes	3,426
Shamrock Interiors	4,629

(c) **Reconcile the balances shown above with the sales ledger control account balance you have calculated in part (a).**

	£
Sales ledger control account balance as at 30 June	
Total of subsidiary (sales) ledger accounts as at 30 June	
Difference	

(d) **Which TWO of the following reasons could be explanations of why the total on a sales ledger control account may be higher than the total of balances on a sales ledger?**

✓

Sales returns may have been omitted from the subsidiary ledger.	
Discounts allowed may have been omitted from the subsidiary ledger.	
Sales returns may have been entered in the subsidiary ledger twice.	
Discounts allowed may have been entered in the subsidiary ledger twice.	

It is important to reconcile the sales ledger control account on a regular basis.

(e) **Which of the following statements is true?**

	✓
Reconciliation of the sales ledger control account assures managers that the amount showing as owed to suppliers is correct.	
Reconciliation of the sales ledger control account assures managers that the amount showing as outstanding from customers is correct.	
Reconciliation of the sales ledger control account will show if a purchase invoice has been omitted from the purchase ledger.	
Reconciliation of the sales ledger control account will show if a purchase invoice has been omitted from the sales ledger.	

102 JACK'S BOX

This is a summary of transactions with customers of Jack's Box during the month of April.

(a) **Show whether each entry will be a debit or a credit in the Sales ledger control account in the General ledger.**

Details	Amount £	Debit ✓	Credit ✓
Balance of receivables at 1 April	60,589		
Goods sold on credit	26,869		
Payments received from credit customers	29,411		
Discount allowed	598		
Goods returned from credit customers	1,223		

(b) **What will be the balance brought down on 1 May on the above account?**

	✓
Dr £55,030	
Cr £55,030	
Dr £56,226	
Cr £56,226	
Dr £52,584	
Cr £52,584	

The following debit balances were in the subsidiary (receivables) ledger on 1 May.

	£
Olsen & Lane	19,455
Frith Ltd	625
Hodgetts & Co	412
Geevor plc	17,623
Trevaskis Farm Ltd	16,888

(c)   **Reconcile the balances shown above with the sales ledger control account balance you have calculated in part (b).**

	£
Sales Ledger control account balances as at 30 April	
Total of subsidiary (sales) ledger accounts as at 30 April	
Difference	

(d)   **What may have caused the difference of £1,223 you calculated in part (c)?**

	✓
Sales returns may have been omitted from the subsidiary ledger	
Discounts allowed have been omitted from the subsidiary ledger	
Sales returns have been entered into the subsidiary ledger twice	
Discounts allowed have been entered into subsidiary ledger twice	

It is important to reconcile the sales ledger control account on a regular basis.

(e)   **Which of the following statements is true?**

	✓
Reconciliation of the sales ledger control account will show if a purchase invoice has been omitted from the purchases ledger.	
Reconciliation of the sales ledger control account will show if a sales invoice has been omitted from the purchases ledger.	
Reconciliation of the sales ledger control account assures managers that the amount showing due to suppliers is correct.	
Reconciliation of the sales ledger control account assures managers that the amount showing due from customers is correct.	

101 ZHANG

When Zhang came to reconcile his SLCA with his list of balances on the sales ledger, he found that they did not match. The SLCA had a balance of £65,830 and the list of balances totalled £65,090. Upon further investigation, he discovered that the following errors had been made:

1   The sales day book had been incorrectly totalled and had been overcast by £1,200.

2   A contra of £800 had been made in the SLCA, but had not been recorded in the sales ledger.

3   A credit note of £130 had been posted twice in the sales ledger.

4   A discount given of £210 had only been recorded in the sales ledger.

(a) **Update the SLCA and list of balances to make sure that the two agree.**

SLCA

Details	Amount £	Details	Amount £
Balance b/d	65,830		
		Balance c/d	
Balance b/d			

List of balances:

	£
Total	65,090
Revised total	

(b) **Show whether the following statements are true or false:**

	True ✓	False ✓
An aged trade receivables analysis is used when chasing customers for outstanding payments.		
An aged trade receivables analysis is sent to credit customers when payments are being requested.		

104 HANDYSIDE

When Handyside came to reconcile his PLCA with his list of balances on the purchases ledger, he found that they did not match. The PLCA had a balance of £25,360 and the list of balances totalled £26,000. Upon further investigation, he discovered that the following errors had been made:

1   In the list of balances, a purchase of £2,400 had been entered at the net amount.

2   Returns of £350 had not been applied to the purchases ledger.

3   An invoice for £600 plus VAT had not been posted in the general ledger yet.

4   Returns of £120 were missing from the PLCA.

5   An invoice for £340 had been entered into the purchases ledger as £430.

(a) **Update the PLCA and list of balances to make sure that the two agree.**

PLCA

Details	Amount £	Details	Amount £
		Balance b/d	25,360
Balance c/d			
		Balance b/d	

List of balances:

	£
Total	26,000
Revised total	

(b) **Show whether the following statements are true or false:**

	True ✓	False ✓
The purchases ledger control account enables a business to see how much is owed to individual suppliers		
The purchases ledger control account total should reconcile to the total of the list of supplier balances in the purchases ledger		

105   RING RING TELEPHONE

The following is an extract from Ring Ring Telephone's books of prime entry.

Totals for quarter			
Sales day-book		**Purchases day-book**	
Net:	£153,000	Net:	£81,000
VAT:	£30,600	VAT:	£16,200
Gross:	£183,600	Gross:	£97,200
Sales returns day-book		**Purchases returns day-book**	
Net:	£1,800	Net:	£5,800
VAT:	£360	VAT:	£1,160
Gross:	£2,160	Gross:	£6,960
Cash book			
Net cash sales:	£240		
VAT:	£48		
Gross cash sales:	£288		

(a)   **What will be the entries in the VAT control account to record the VAT transactions in the quarter?**

VAT control

Details	Amount £	Details	Amount £

Picklist: Cash sales, Purchases, Purchases returns, Sales, Sales returns, VAT.

The VAT return has been completed and shows an amount owing from HM Revenue and Customs of £15,248.

(b)   **Is the VAT return correct?**   Yes/No

(c)   At the end of the next period, the VAT control account has debit entries amounting to £93,800 and credit entries amounting to £54,400.

The following transactions have not yet been recorded in the VAT control account:

VAT of £400 on purchase of equipment
VAT of £900 on cash sales

What will be the balance brought down on the VAT account after the transactions above have been recorded? Also identify whether the balance will be a debit or a credit.

	£	*Debit*	*Credit*
Balance brought down			

106   PHILIP'S CABINS

The following is an extract from Philip's Cabins books of prime entry.

Totals for quarter			
Sales day-book		**Purchases day-book**	
Net:	£179,800	Net:	£100,200
VAT:	£35,960	VAT:	£20,040
Gross:	£215,760	Gross:	£120,240
Sales returns day-book		**Purchases returns day-book**	
Net:	£3,000	Net:	£5,720
VAT:	£600	VAT:	£1,144
Gross:	£3,600	Gross:	£6,864
Cash book			
Net cash sales:	£560		
VAT:	£112		
Gross cash sales:	£672		

(a)   **What will be the entries in the VAT control account to record the VAT transactions in the quarter?**

VAT control

Details	Amount £	Details	Amount £

Picklist: Cash sales, Purchases, Purchases returns, Sales, Sales returns, VAT.

The VAT return has been completed and shows an amount due to HM Revenue and Customs of £14,540.

(b)   **Is the VAT return correct?**   Yes/No

107 DISLEY

(a) **Show whether each item is a debit or credit balance in the VAT control account by copying the amount into the correct column.**

	£	*Debit*	*Credit*
VAT total in the sales day book	65,420		
VAT total in the purchases day book	21,340		
VAT total in the sales returns day book	480		
VAT balance brought forward, owed to HMRC	24,910		
VAT on irrecoverable debts	830		
VAT on petty cash expenses paid	210		

The VAT return has been completed and shows an amount due to HM Revenue and Customs of £67,740.

(b) **Is the VAT return correct?** Yes/No

(c) At the end of the next period, the VAT control account has debit entries amounting to £42,300 and credit entries amounting to £61,250.

The following transactions have not yet been recorded in the VAT control account:

VAT total in the discounts received day book of £980

VAT of £200 on an irrecoverable debt

What will be the balance brought down on the VAT account after the transactions above have been recorded? Also identify whether the balance will be a debit or a credit.

	£	*Debit*	*Credit*
Balance brought down			

108 AWESOME LTD

You are told that the opening inventory of a single raw material in the stores is 6,000 units at £6 per unit. During the month, another 6,000 units at £10 were received and the following week 7,150 units were issued.

Task 1

Identify the valuation method described in the statements below:

Characteristic	*FIFO*	*LIFO*	*AVCO*
• Closing inventory is valued at £48,500.			
• The issue of inventory is valued at £57,200.			
• The issue of inventory is valued at £66,900.			

Task 2

Identify whether the statements in the table below are true or false by putting a tick in the relevant column.

	True	False
• FIFO values the issue of inventory at £47,500.		
• AVCO values the closing inventory at £38,400.		
• LIFO values the closing inventory at £29,100.		

109 AMAZING LTD

You are told that the opening inventory of a single raw material in the stores is 2,000 units at £1.50 per unit. During the month, another 5,000 units at £5 were received and the following week 6,000 units were issued.

Task 1

Identify the valuation method described in the statements below:

Characteristic	FIFO	LIFO	AVCO
• Closing inventory is valued at £1,500.			
• The issue of inventory is valued at £23,000.			
• The issue of inventory is valued at £24,000.			

Task 2

Identify whether the statements in the table below are true or false by putting a tick in the relevant column.

	True	False
• LIFO values the issue of inventory at £26,500.		
• AVCO values the closing inventory at £5,000.		
• LIFO values the closing inventory at £4,000.		

110 STONE LTD

Stone Ltd sells stone to builders. It had the following movements in one type of stone for the month of June.

DATE	RECEIPTS		ISSUES	
	Tonnes	Cost	Tonnes	Cost
June 1	500	£7,500		
June 8	350	£6,125		
June 15	275	£4,950		
June 22			650	
June 29	500	£8,750		

Complete the table below for the issue and closing inventory values, stating your answers to the nearest pound.

Method	Cost of issue on 22 June	Closing inventory at 30 June
FIFO	£	£
LIFO	£	£
AVCO	£	£

111 NATAL LTD

Natal Ltd makes and sells a wide range of clothes for babies. The following is an inventory card for Natal's most popular product for the month of December.

DATE	RECEIPTS		ISSUES	
	Units	Cost	Units	Cost
December 3	10,000	£85,000		
December 18	14,000	£112,000		
December 19	50,000	£350,000		
December 25			72,500	
December 29	5,000	£30,000		

Task 1

Complete the table below for the issue and closing inventory values. Give your answers to the nearest pound.

Method	Cost of issue on 25 Dec	Closing inventory at 29 Dec
LIFO	£	£
AVCO	£	£

Task 2

Identify the following statements as true or false by putting a tick in the relevant column of the table below:

	True	False
• FIFO would give a lower closing inventory valuation on the 29 December than LIFO and AVCO.		
• FIFO would give a lower cost of issue on the 25 December than LIFO and AVCO.		

112 GANDALF LTD

Gandalf Ltd has the following movements in a certain type of inventory into and out of its stores for the month of July.

DATE	RECEIPTS			ISSUES			BALANCE
	Units	Unit cost	Total £	Units	Unit cost	Total £	Total £
July 2	600	£1.50	£900				
July 4	500	£1.70	£850				
July 15				620			
July 19	200	£1.80	£360				
July 31				400			

Calculate the costs of the issues made on July 15 and July 31 if Gandalf plc uses a LIFO inventory valuation method.

	Valuation £
• July 15	
• July 31	

113 NULAB LTD

Identify the labour payment method by putting a tick in the relevant column of the table below:

Payment method	Time-rate	Piecework	Piece-rate plus bonus
• Labour is paid based solely on the production achieved.			
• Labour is paid extra if an agreed level of output is exceeded.			
• Labour is paid according to hours worked.			

114 MANDELA LTD

Identify whether the following statements are true or false in the relevant column of the table below:

Statement	True	False
• Time rate is paid based on the production achieved.		
• Overtime is paid for hours worked over the standard hours agreed.		
• Piece rate is paid according to hours worked.		

115 PERRES LTD

Identify the hourly payment method by putting a tick in the relevant column of the table below:

Payment method	Basic rate	Overtime premium	Overtime rate
• This is the amount paid above the basic rate for hours worked in excess of the normal hours.			
• This is the total amount paid per hour for hours worked in excess of the normal hours.			
• This is the amount paid per hour for normal hours worked.			

116 TEVEZ LTD

Identify the following statements as true or false by putting a tick in the relevant column of the table below:

Statement	True	False
• Direct labour costs can be identified with the goods being made or the service being provided.		
• Indirect labour costs vary directly with the level of activity.		

117 BERDYCH LTD

Identify the whether the labour payment is usually associated with a fixed or variable cost by putting a tick in the relevant column of the table below:

Payment method	Variable	Fixed
• Labour that is paid based on a time rate basis per hour worked.		
• Labour is paid on a monthly salary basis.		
• Labour that is based on number of units produced.		

118 PIECEWORK STATEMENTS

Identify the following statements as either true or false by putting a tick in the relevant column of the table below:

Statement	True	False
• Piecework encourages employees to work harder.		
• Piecework requires accurate recording of the number of hours staff have worked.		
• Piecework encourages workers to improve the quality of the units they produce.		

119 PHOENIX LTD

Phoenix plc pays its employees £8.00 per hour and expects them to make 20 units per hour. Any excess production will be paid a bonus of £1.50 per unit.

Identify the following statements as being true or false by putting a tick in the relevant column of the table below:

Statement	True	False
An employee who works 38 hours and makes 775 units will not receive a bonus.		
An employee who works 40 hours and makes 815 units will receive total pay of £342.50.		
An employee who works 37 hours and makes 744 units will earn a bonus of £6.		

120 KAHN LTD

Kahn Ltd uses a time-rate method with bonus to pay its direct labour in one of its factories. The time-rate used is £12 per hour and a worker is expected to produce 5 units an hour, any time saved is paid at £6 per hour.

Calculate the gross wage for the week including bonus for the three workers in the table below:

Worker	Hours worked	Units produced	Basic wage	Bonus	Gross wage
A. Smith	35	175	£	£	£
J. O'Hara	35	180	£	£	£
M. Stizgt	35	185	£	£	£

121 ENTERPRISE LTD

Enterprise Ltd pays a time-rate of £12 per hour to its direct labour force for a standard 35 hour week. Any of the labour force working in excess of 35 hours is paid an overtime rate of time and a half.

Calculate the gross wage for the week for the three workers in the table below:

Worker	Hours worked	Basic wage	Overtime	Gross wage
J. Picard	37 hours	£	£	£
B. Crusher	42 hours	£	£	£
D. Troi	31 hours	£	£	£

122 SGC LTD

SGC Ltd uses a basic salary plus piecework method to pay labour in one of its factories. The basic salary is £285 per week the piece rate used is £0.75 per unit produced.

Calculate the gross wage for the week for the two workers in the table below. Enter your answer to the nearest penny.

Worker	Units produced in week	Gross wage
J. O'Neill	500 units	£
S. Carter	650 units	£

123 GOTHIC LTD

Gothic Ltd uses a time-rate method with bonus to pay its direct labour in one of its factories. The time-rate used is £17 per hour and a worker is expected to produce 8 units an hour, anything over this and the worker is paid a bonus of £5 per unit.

Calculate the gross wage for the week including bonus for the three workers in the table below:

Worker	Hours worked	Units produced	Basic wage	Bonus	Gross wage
M. Shelley	37	300	£	£	£
G. Leroux	37	312	£	£	£
E. A. Poe	37	296	£	£	£

124 AVENGERS LTD

Avengers Ltd pays a time-rate of £10 per hour to its direct labour force a standard 35 hour week. Any of the labour force working in excess of this over the four week period is paid an overtime rate of time and a quarter.

Calculate the gross wage for the **4-week** period for the three workers in the table below. Enter your answers to the nearest pound.

Worker	Hours worked	Basic wage	Overtime	Gross wage
T. Stark	138	£	£	£
B. Banner	142	£	£	£
S. Rogers	145	£	£	£

125 DRACO LTD

Draco Ltd uses a piecework method to pay labour in one of its factories. The rate used is 80p per unit produced up to the standard number of units to be produced per week of 250. For any units over that the workers will get £10 per 20 units.

Calculate the gross wage for the week for the three workers in the table below:

Worker	Units produced in week	Gross wage
P. Jones	240 units	£
D. Bannatyne	350 units	£
L. Redford	250 units	£

126 JLA PLC

JLA plc pays its employees £5 per hour and expects them to make 6 units per hour. Any time saved will be paid as a bonus at £8 per hour.

Identify the following statements as being true or false by putting a tick in the relevant column of the table below:

Statement	True	False
During a 30 hour week, an employee producing 192 units would receive a bonus of £16.		
During a 35 hour week, an employee producing 240 units would receive total pay of £215.		
During a 30 hour week, an employee producing 180 units would not receive a bonus.		

127 INJUSTICE LTD

Davidson Ltd pays a basic wage of £175/week plus £1.20 per unit produced.

Calculate the gross wage for the week for the three workers in the table below:

Worker	Units produced	Basic wage	Piece work	Gross wage
N. Wing	295	£	£	£
W. Woman	355	£	£	£
T. Flash	385	£	£	£

128   GREENWOOD LTD

Greenwood Ltd pays a basic wage of £350/week equivalent to a time-rate of £10 per hour and a standard 35 hour week. Workers are expected to produce 5 units an hour and for units produced in excess of this a bonus is paid based on £7 for every hour saved.

So, for example, if 10 additional units are produced, then this would be equivalent to two hours saved and a bonus of £14 awarded.

Calculate the gross wage for the week including bonus for the three workers in the table below:

Worker	Hours worked	Units produced	Basic wage	Bonus	Gross wage
B. Ryan	35	175	£	£	£
S. Chang	35	190	£	£	£
E. Schneider	35	210	£	£	£

129   DOOMSDAY LTD

Doomsday Ltd is costing a single product which has the following cost details:

Variable costs per unit	Per unit	Cost
Materials	45kg	£0.50/kg
Labour	2.5hrs	£16/hour

Total fixed costs

Production overhead	£75,000
Administration overhead	£110,000
Sales and distribution	£75,000

Complete the following total cost and unit cost table for a production level of 20,000 units. Overheads are absorbed on a cost per unit basis. Give your answer to the nearest penny for the unit cost and the nearest pound for total cost.

Element	Total cost for 20,000 units	Unit cost
Direct costs	£	£
Production overhead	£	£
Non production overhead	£	£
Total costs	£	£

130 OLSEN LTD

Olsen Ltd is costing a single product which has the following cost details:

Variable costs	Per unit
Materials	£12
Labour	£17

Total Fixed Costs

Production overhead   £80,000

Administration overhead   £40,000

Complete the following total cost and unit cost table for a production level of 80,000 units. Give your answer to the nearest penny for the unit cost and the nearest pound for total cost.

Element	Total cost	Unit cost
Materials	£	£
Labour	£	£
Production overheads	£	£
Administration overheads	£	£
Total	£	£

131 CORONATION LTD

Coronation Ltd is costing a single product which has the following cost details

Variable costs	Per unit	Cost
Materials	50g	£10/kg
Labour	1hr	£6/hour

Total fixed costs

Production overhead   £40,000

Administration overhead   £20,000

Sales and distribution   £25,000

Complete the following total cost and unit cost table for a production level of 5,000 units. Overheads are absorbed on a cost per unit basis. Give your answer to the nearest penny for the unit cost and the nearest pound for total cost.

Element	Total cost for 5,000 units	Unit cost
Direct costs	£	£
Production overhead	£	£
Non production overhead	£	£
Total costs	£	£

132 LUTHOR LTD

Luthor Ltd makes a single product and for a production level of 15,000 units has the following cost details:

Materials	60,000kg	at £15/kilo
Labour	37,500hrs	at £9/hour
Fixed overheads		£570,000

Complete the table below to show the unit cost at the production level of 15,000 units. Overheads are absorbed on a cost per unit basis. Give your answer to the nearest penny.

Element	Unit cost
Materials	£
Labour	£
Fixed overheads	£
Total	£

133 WILKINSON LTD

Wilkinson Ltd is looking to calculate the unit cost for one of the products it makes. It needs to calculate an overhead absorption rate to apply to each unit. The methods it is considering are a rate per machine hour, a rate per labour hour, and a rate per unit.

Total factory activity is forecast as follows:

Machine hours	10,000
Labour hours	12,500
Units	60,000
Overheads	£150,000

Task 1

Complete the table below to show the possible overhead absorption rates that Wilkinson Ltd could use. The absorption rates should be calculated to two decimal places.

	Machine hour	Labour hour	Unit
Overheads (£)			
Activity			
Absorption rate (£)			

Task 2

The following data relates to making one unit of the product:

Material	2 kilos at £5 per kilo
Labour	15 minutes at £10 per hour
Production time	10 minutes

Complete the table below (to two decimal places) to calculate the total unit cost, using the three overhead absorption rates you have calculated in task 1.

Cost	Machine hour (£)	Labour hour (£)	Unit (£)
Material			
Labour			
Direct cost			
Overheads			
Total unit cost			

134 HODGSON LTD

Hodgson Ltd is looking to calculate the unit cost for one of the products it makes. It needs to calculate an overhead absorption rate to apply to each unit. The methods it is considering are a rate per machine hour, a rate per labour hour, and a rate per unit.

Total factory activity is forecast as follows:

Machine hours	15,000
Labour hours	20,000
Units	100,000
Overheads	£250,000

Task 1

Complete the table below to show the possible overhead absorption rates that Hodgson Ltd could use. The absorption rates should be calculated to two decimal places.

	Machine hour	Labour hour	Unit
Overheads (£)			
Activity			
Absorption rate (£)			

Task 2

The following data relates to making one unit of the product:

Material	4 kilos at £6 per kilo
Labour	30 minutes at £12 per hour
Production time	20 minutes

Complete the table below (to two decimal places) to calculate the total unit cost, using the three overhead absorption rates you have calculated in task 1.

Cost	Machine hour (£)	Labour hour (£)	Unit (£)
Material			
Labour			
Direct cost			
Overheads			
Total unit cost			

135   BARNES LTD

Barnes Ltd is looking to calculate the unit cost for one of the products it makes. It needs to calculate an overhead absorption rate to apply to each unit. The methods it is considering are a rate per machine hour, a rate per labour hour, and a rate per unit.

Total factory activity is forecast as follows:

Machine hours	17,500
Labour hours	12,000
Units	40,000
Overheads	£130,000

Task 1

Complete the table below to show the possible overhead absorption rates that Barnes Ltd could use. The absorption rates should be calculated to two decimal places.

	Machine hour	Labour hour	Unit
Overheads (£)			
Activity			
Absorption rate (£)			

Task 2

The following data relates to making one unit of the product:

Material	3 kilos at £5 per kilo
Labour	20 minutes at £15 per hour
Production time	30 minutes

Complete the table below (to two decimal places) to calculate the total unit cost, using the three overhead absorption rates you have calculated in task 1.

Cost	Machine hour (£)	Labour hour (£)	Unit (£)
Material			
Labour			
Direct cost			
Overheads			
Total unit cost			

136 ANDREW LTD

Andrew Ltd is looking to calculate the unit cost for one of the products it makes. It needs to calculate an overhead absorption rate to apply to each unit. The methods it is considering are a rate per machine hour, a rate per labour hour, and a rate per unit.

Total factory activity is forecast as follows:

Machine hours	9,000
Labour hours	11,000
Units	60,000
Overheads	£145,000

Task 1

Complete the table below to show the possible overhead absorption rates that Andrew Ltd could use. The absorption rates should be calculated to two decimal places.

	Machine hour	Labour hour	Unit
Overheads (£)			
Activity			
Absorption rate (£)			

Task 2

The following data relates to making one unit of the product:

Material	1 kilo at £8 per kilo
Labour	30 minutes at £14 per hour
Production time	20 minutes

Complete the table below (to two decimal places) to calculate the total unit cost, using the three overhead absorption rates you have calculated in task 1.

Cost	Machine hour (£)	Labour hour (£)	Unit (£)
Material			
Labour			
Direct cost			
Overheads			
Total unit cost			

137   JOKER LTD

Reorder the following costs into a manufacturing account format on the right side of the table below for the year ended 31 December.

	£		£
Closing inventory of work in progress	52,000		
Direct labour	140,000		
Opening inventory of raw materials	50,000		
Closing inventory of finished goods	61,000		
Closing inventory of raw materials	65,000		
Manufacturing overheads	85,000		
COST OF GOODS SOLD	322,000		
MANUFACTURING COST	330,000		
Purchases of raw materials	120,000		
Opening inventory of work in progress	48,000		
Opening inventory of finished goods	57,000		
DIRECT COST	245,000		
DIRECT MATERIALS USED	105,000		
COST OF GOODS MANUFACTURED	326,000		

Enter the correct figures for the following costs which were not provided in the table above.

	£
DIRECT MATERIALS USED	
DIRECT COST	
MANUFACTURING COST	
COST OF GOODS MANUFACTURED	
COST OF GOODS SOLD	

138 RIDDLER LTD

Reorder the following costs into a manufacturing account format on the right side of the table below for the year ended 31 May. Enter the correct figures for the costs in bold that are not provided.

	£		£
DIRECT COST			
Closing inventory of raw materials	20,000		
Closing inventory of work in progress	20,000		
Opening inventory of finished goods	60,000		
Direct labour	194,000		
Closing inventory of finished goods	50,000		
Manufacturing overheads	106,000		
Purchases of raw materials	100,000		
Opening inventory of work in progress	16,000		
COST OF GOODS SOLD			
DIRECT MATERIALS USED			
Opening inventory of raw materials	14,000		
MANUFACTURING COST			
COST OF GOODS MANUFACTURED			

139 BOOKWORM LTD

Reorder the following costs into a manufacturing account format on the right side of the table below for the year ended 31 December. Enter the correct figures for the costs in bold that are not provided.

	£		£
DIRECT COST			
Direct labour	15,000		
MANUFACTURING COST			
Opening inventory of raw materials	5,000		
Closing inventory of finished goods	16,000		
Purchases of raw materials	15,000		
DIRECT MATERIALS USED			
Manufacturing overheads	25,000		
Closing inventory of raw materials	8,000		
COST OF GOODS SOLD			
COST OF GOODS MANUFACTURED			
Opening inventory of finished goods	12,000		
Opening inventory of work in progress	4,000		
Closing inventory of work in progress	6,000		

140   VARIOUS LTD

Identify the following statements as being true or false by putting a tick in the relevant column of the table below:

Statement	True	False
A variance is the difference between budgeted and actual cost		
A favourable variance occurs when actual costs are less than budgeted.		
An adverse variance occurs when actual income is less than budgeted.		
A favourable variance occurs when actual income is the same as budgeted income.		

141   JONES LTD

Identify the following statements as being true or false by putting a tick in the relevant column of the table below:

Statement	True	False
If budgeted sales are 6,000 units at £7.50 per unit and actual sales are £47,600, the sales variance is favourable		
A favourable cost variance occurs when an actual cost of £9,800 is compared to a budgeted cost of £24 per unit for a budgeted output of 400 units		
A variance arises from a comparison of budgeted costs for last year with actual costs for this year		
If actual material costs are the same as budgeted costs for materials then no variance arises		

142   LANCASTER LTD

Identify the following statements as being true or false by putting a tick in the relevant column of the table below:

Statement	True	False
If budgeted sales are 14,000 units at £3.50 per unit and actual sales are £45,200, the sales variance is favourable		
An adverse cost variance occurs when an actual cost of £68,400 is compared to a budgeted cost of £14 per unit for a budgeted output of 5,000 units		
A variance arises from a comparison of budgeted costs for this year with actual costs for this year		
If actual material costs are the same as budgeted costs for materials then the materials variance is favourable		

143 GOODE LTD

Identify the following statements as being true or false by putting a tick in the relevant column of the table below:

Statement	True	False
The variance for the Direct Material cost of Department B should be reported to the purchasing manager		
The variance for the Direct Labour cost for Department A should be reported to the sales manager		
The variance for the Direct Labour cost for Department B should be reported to the production manager of Department A		
A Direct Material cost variance that has been deemed Not Significant should not be reported		

144 BROWN LTD

Identify the following statements as being true or false by putting a tick in the relevant column of the table below:

Statement	True	False
The variance for the Direct Material cost of Department A should be reported to the purchasing manager		
The variance for the Direct Labour cost for Department A should be reported to the production manager of Department B		
The variance for sales should be reported to the sales manager		
A Direct Material cost variance that has been deemed Significant should not be reported		

145 BLUEBELL LTD

The following performance report for this month has been produced for Bluebell Ltd as summarised in the table below.

Calculate the variances in the table below and indicate whether they are adverse or favourable by putting an A or F in the relevant column and calculate the variance as a % to the nearest whole number.

Cost type	Budget £	Actual £	Variance £	Adverse/ Favourable	%
Sales	£204,555	£197,455			
Direct materials	£39,000	£42,300			
Direct labour	£75,000	£83,000			
Production overheads	£69,000	£64,800			
Administration overheads	£53,000	£58,900			

146 TRIUMPH LTD

Task 1

Identify the type of cost behaviour (fixed, variable or semi-variable) described in each statement by ticking the relevant boxes in the table below.

Statement	Fixed	Variable	Semi-variable
At 9,000 units this cost is £29,250, and at 12,000 units it is £39,000			
At 5,000 units this cost is £5.20 per unit, and at 8,000 units it is £3.25 per unit			
At 19,800 units, this cost is £64,500, and at 27,000 units it is £82,500			

Task 2

Complete the table below by inserting all costs for activity levels of 6,000 and 14,000.

	6,000 units	7,000 units	10,000 units	14,000 units
Variable cost (£)				
Fixed cost (£)				
Total cost (£)		45,000	54,000	

147   BUNGLE LTD

Bungle Ltd usually produces 9,000 units but is planning to increase production to 14,000 units during the next period.

Identify the following statements as either true or false by putting a tick in the relevant column of the table below:

Statement	True	False
Total variable costs will decrease.		
Total fixed costs will remain the same.		
The variable cost per unit will remain the same.		
The fixed cost per unit will increase.		

148   TF

Identify the following statements as either true or false by putting a tick in the relevant column of the table below:

Statement	True	False
Variable costs change directly with changes in activity.		
Fixed costs change directly with changes in activity		
Stepped costs are fixed within a set range of output.		

149 GLACIER

Glacier has a corporate commitment to improving the local environment and has implemented a number of initiatives, such as maximising the use of recyclable materials in its manufacturing processes. Additionally, Glaciers' Corporate Social Responsibility Team organised an event, a 'three-drop challenge' which required a sponsored team to abseil down the side of three local high-rise buildings.

The challenge required that the CSR Team obtained a licence from the local public authority to close a road and divert traffic whilst the event took place. The cost of the licence was estimated to be £1,500. It was also estimated that the sponsorship funds that would be raised from the event would be £25,000. The CSR team is responsible for reporting on the costs incurred and funds raised from the event. The sponsorship proceeds raised would be donated to a local charity.

The licence was obtained prior to the event taking place at a cost of £1,250. The sponsorship funds raised were £27,200. You have been asked to compare the budgeted costs and funds raised with the actual results by completing the table below.

Complete the table below by:

- Inserting the budgeted amount for each item

- Inserting the actual amount for each item

- Inserting the variance for each item

- Selecting whether each variance is adverse or favourable.

▽ Drop down list for task:

| Adverse |
| Favourable |

Event performance report				
Cost	**Budget** **(£)**	**Actual** **(£)**	**Variance** **(£)**	**Adverse/** **Favourable**
Licence cost				▽
Funds				
Sponsorship funds raised				▽

150 BERLINE

Berline has a corporate commitment to improving the local environment, and has implemented a number of initiatives, such as setting targets to minimise wastage resulting from its production processes. Additionally, The Corporate Social Responsibility Team at Berline organised a fund-raising event, a charity football match, to which members of the public would pay an admission fee, the proceeds of which would be donated to a local charity.

Amongst other things, the event required that a sports centre be hired, and that refreshments would be available for spectators to purchase during the event. It was estimated that 1,000 spectators would attend the event and that the cost of providing refreshments would be £2 per spectator. A commemorative souvenir magazine of the event would be produced and given to each spectator at a budgeted cost £1 per spectator. The CSR team is responsible for reporting on the costs of the event.

The actual cost of providing the refreshments was £2,250 and the actual cost of producing the souvenir magazine was £950. You have been asked to compare the actual costs with the budgeted costs and to identify whether any variance calculated is significant, that is in excess of 4% of budget.

Complete the table below by:

- Inserting the budgeted amount for each item

- Inserting the actual amount for each item

- Inserting the variance for each item

- Selecting whether each variance is adverse or favourable

- Selected whether each variance is significant or not.

∇ Drop down list for task :

Adverse	Yes
Favourable	No

Event cost performance report					
Cost	**Budget** (£)	**Actual** (£)	**Variance** (£)	**Adverse/ Favourable**	**Significant**
Refreshments				∇	∇
Magazine				∇	∇

Section 4

PRACTICE QUESTIONS

AO4 COMMUNICATE FINANCIAL INFORMATION EFFECTIVELY

151 MRS MAY

This is a draft letter to be addressed to Mrs May, of MayMe Ltd, a supplier, regarding the incorrect amount being recorded on an invoice.

Review the letter and identify FIVE words which are spelled incorrectly, or are inappropriate.

Hi Mrs May,

Please find enclosed a copy of the invoice received from MayMe Ltd for a recent purchase.

The unit price stated on the invoice is incorrect. The unit price wos quoted at £36 per unit on the purchase order, yet we have been invoiced £63 per unit.

Pleaze credit this invoice and reissue with the correct amount of £36 per unit. One we have received the corrected invoice, we can make payment.

Yours faithfully

---

152 BILLY

Below is a response to a customer complaint.

Please highlight five words that are spelt incorrectly, or are inappropriate:

Dear Billy,

I was very cheesed to here that you did not receive your goods in proper working order. We have very strict internal procedures, which are designed to prevent faulty goods reaching our customers. Please rest assured that we are investigating fully you're case and are striving to ensure that this does not happen again in the future.

By way of an apolojy we will be refunding you in full and offering you a 20% discount off your next purchase.

Kind regards

John Anderson

Store manager

---

153 MR CADBURY

Review the draft correspondence below highlighting the spelling errors and inappropriate wording used.

Dear Mr Cadbury

I enclose a copy of the invoice which your requested during are telephone conversation this morning.

Please note this invoice is dated 31 June and therefor is overdue for payment.

I look forward to receiving your cheque in full settlement by return of post.

Yours faithfully

154 JEEPERS LTD

(a) **Indicate whether each of the following costs are direct or not by putting a tick in the relevant column of the table below:**

Cost	Yes	No
Materials used in production.		
Piecework labour costs.		
Salary of chief executive.		

Jeepers Ltd makes a single product. At a production level of 15,000 units, the company has the following costs:

Materials	37,500 kilos at £14.00 per kilo
Labour	7,500 hours at £16.00 per hour
Overheads	£570,000

(b) **Complete the table below to show the unit product cost at the production level of 15,000 units. Overheads are absorbed on a cost per unit basis. Give your answer to the nearest pound.**

Element	Unit product cost
Materials	£
Labour	£
Direct cost	£
Overheads	£
Total	£

155 GLORIA LTD

Gloria Ltd is costing a single product which has the following cost details:

Variable costs per unit

Materials	£2
Labour	£3
Royalties	£0.50

Total fixed costs

Production overhead	£80,000
Sales and distribution	£90,000

(a) **Complete the following total cost and unit cost table for a production level of 20,000 units. Give your answer to the nearest penny for the unit cost and the nearest pound for the total cost.**

Element	Unit cost	Total cost for 20,000 units
Variable production costs	£	£
Fixed production costs	£	£
Total production cost	£	£

(b) **In the box below, write notes in preparation for a meeting you will have with your manager, including:**

- **a brief introduction outlining the areas you will discuss**

- **an explanation of what a fixed production cost is, including an example of a fixed production cost**

- **an example of what a variable production cost is, including an example of a variable production cost**

- **an explanation of what happens to fixed and variable production costs if output is increased from 20,000 to 25,000 units.**

Your notes must be sufficiently detailed, clearly written and well-structured as they will be a formal record of your meeting discussion.

156 BIZARRO LTD

Bizarro Ltd makes a single product and for a production level of 17,000 units has the following cost details:

	Per unit	Cost
Materials	2.5kg	£18/kilo
Labour	1.0hrs	£9/hour
Fixed overheads		£42,500

(a) **Complete the table below to show the unit cost and total cost at the production level of 17,000 units. Overheads are absorbed on a cost per unit basis. Give your answer to the nearest penny for the unit cost and the nearest pound for total cost.**

Element	Unit cost	Total cost
Materials	£	£
Labour	£	£
Overheads	£	£
Total	£	£

(b) **In the box below, write notes in preparation for a meeting you will have with your supervisor regarding different methods of paying employees including:**

- **a brief introduction outlining the areas you will discuss**

- **an explanation of what a basic pay is, including an example of basic pay**

- **an example of what bonus pay is, including an example of bonus pay**

- **an explanation of what overtime pay is, including an example of overtime pay.**

Your notes must be sufficiently detailed, clearly written and well-structured as they will be a formal record of your meeting discussion.

157 VINNY LTD

Vinny Ltd is a commercial laundrette below are the costings for 15,000 units:

Variable costs

Materials	£75,000
Labour	£120,000

Fixed costs

Production overhead	£100,000

Complete the following total cost and unit cost table for a REVISED production level of 20,000 units. Give your answer to the nearest penny for the unit cost and the nearest pound for total cost.

Element	Unit cost	Total cost
Materials	£	£
Labour	£	£
Overheads	£	£
Total	£	£

158 DARKSEID LTD

Darkseid Ltd makes a single product and for a production level of 95,000 units has the following cost details:

Materials	47,500kg	at £7/kilo
Labour	71,250hrs	at £9/hour
Fixed overheads		£242,000

Complete the table below to show the unit cost at a REVISED production level of 100,000 units. Overheads are absorbed on a cost per unit basis. Give your answer to the nearest penny.

Element	Unit cost
Materials	£
Labour	£
Fixed overheads	£
Total	£

159 EREBOR PLC

Erebor Ltd has produced a performance report detailing budgeted and actual cost for last month.

(a)   Calculate the amount of the variance for each cost type and then determine whether it is adverse or favourable (enter A or F).

Cost type	Budget £	Actual £	Variance £	Adverse or favourable (A or F)
Sales	600,500	597,800		
Direct materials	205,800	208,500		
Direct labour	155,000	154,800		
Production overheads	65,000	72,100		
Administration overheads	58,400	55,200		

(b)   In the box below, write a brief report for the Warehouse Manager that explains the FIFO, AVCO and LIFO methods of inventory valuations of paying employees including:

Your report must be sufficiently detailed, clearly written and well-structured.

Report to the Warehouse Manager

Methods of inventory valuation

160 BELEGOST LTD

The following performance report for this month has been produced for Belegost Ltd as summarised in the table below. Any variance in excess of 6% of budget is deemed to be significant and should be reported to the relevant manager for review and appropriate action.

(a) **Determine whether the variance for each figure is adverse or favourable by putting an A or F into the relevant column of the table below. Put an S in the relevant column if the variance is significant or an NS if the variance is not significant.**

	Budget £	Actual £	Adverse or Favourable (A or F)	Significant or not significant (S or NS)
Sales	205,000	207,100		
Direct materials	75,150	78,750		
Direct labour	110,556	107,950		
Production overheads	14,190	12,500		
Non-production overheads	16,190	17,880		

(b) **In the box below, write a brief report to the Production Manager which covers the following:**

- **a brief introduction outlining the areas included in your report**

- **an explanation of what a variance is**

- **why only significant variances may be investigated by an organisation.**

Your report must be detailed, clearly written and well-structured.

Report to the Production Manager

Variances and their investigation

161 MORIA LTD

The following performance report for this month has been produced for Moria Ltd. Any variance in excess of 7% of budget is deemed to be significant.

(a) Calculate the variance as a % of the budget and enter your answer into the table below to the nearest whole percentage. Indicate whether the variance is significant or not by entering S for significant and NS for not significant.

Cost type	Budget	Variance	Variance as % of budget	Significant or Not significant
Sales	45,100	4,214		
Material	15,750	1,260		
Labour	12,915	805		
Variable overheads	5,750	315		
Fixed overheads	8,155	1,011		

(b) In the box below, write notes in preparation for a meeting with a colleague from the costing department which explains

- a brief introduction outlining the areas you will discuss

- an explanation of what the direct cost of production is

- an explanation of what the manufacturing cost of production is

Your report must be detailed, clearly written and well-structured.

> **Notes for meeting with colleague**
>
> **Direct cost and manufacturing cost of a product**

Section 5

ANSWERS TO PRACTICE QUESTIONS

ASSESSMENT OBJECTIVE 1

LO1 UNDERSTAND THE FINANCE FUNCTION WITHIN AN ORGANISATION

1 POLICIES AND PROCEDURES

Select THREE policies and procedures from the following list which are likely to apply to the accounting function:

A   Data Protection Act

B   Health and Safety at Work

D   Authorised Signatory Procedure

2 DOCUMENTS

The accounts department of an organisation receives documents and information from other departments.

Match the department with the ONE document they would send to the accounts department:

Department	Document
Purchasing Department	(b) Copy of Purchase order
HR Department	(d) New employee forms
Payroll Department	(e) Statutory Sick pay forms

3 DEPARTMENTS

Match the following departments to **one** information type it would normally use:

Department	Information
Sales Dept	Commission payable to sales staff
Accounts Dept	Cheque book stubs
Payroll Dept	List of all new employees for the period

4   PRINCIPLES

Select THREE principles from the list below that are not a part of the Data Protection Act 1998.

- Information obtained for personal use

- Historic information that is not up to date

- Transferred to other countries without authorisation

5   DATA SECURITY

(a)   Which ONE item would be the best method to back up data from your computer?

- printing out paper copies of everything and filing them away
- make a copy on a removable storage device e.g. DVD, external hard drive
- keep a second copy of the data on your hard disk

(b)   Where should data back-ups from your computer be kept?

- in a separate locked room or off site
- in a drawer near the computer
- on the computer's hard disk

(c)   Which ONE of the following is less likely to damage or delete data?

- archiving
- a virus
- system breakdown

(d)   State three features of a secure password.

- Feature 1 – Do not share your password with others. You should not use a word or phrase of special importance to you—like a birthday or family member.
- Feature 2 – Choose a password that no one will easily guess.
- Feature 3 – Make sure your password is long and consists of letters, numbers and at least one special character

(e)   Which ONE of the following is not a physical control to protect data?

- Restricting access to an office
- Installing an alarm system
- Passwords – this is not a physical control

6   INFORMATION

(a)   **Identify the FOUR key characteristics of useful information from the list below:**

- understandable
- accurate
- legible
- complete
- timely
- credible
- fit for purpose

(b)   **Identify whether each of the following statements is TRUE or FALSE.**

- Only information stated in monetary terms is useful to accountants   – False

- Non-financial information is useful information to individuals who make decisions   – True

7   SERVICE PROVISION

Which TWO of the following services are staff in the finance function most likely to provide to staff in the sales department?

- Conducting job interviews
- Preparing sales brochures
- Budget report analysis
- Photocopier servicing
- Marketing new products
- Payment of sales commission

8   STAKEHOLDERS

Identify which TWO of the following stakeholders a trainee in the finance function is most likely to communicate with.

- People living in houses close to the organisation's Head Office
- The local MP
- HM Revenue & Customs
- The Head teacher of the local school
- Receivables
- An AAT examiner

9   REPORTING LINES

A business employs 2 Directors, 3 Managers and 6 Assistants. Identify who each person should report to by selecting from the picklist.

Person	Should report to the following
Sales and Purchase Ledger Assistant	Accounts department manager
Administration Assistant	General manager
3 Sales Assistants	Sales manager
Payroll Assistant	Accounts department manager
Accounting Department Manager	Finance director

10   PERSON AND ROLE

Match which **one** person each role must report to:

Role	Reports to
Accounts assistant	Accounting department manager
Sales Ledger clerk	Accounting department manager
Machine operator	Factory manager

11   COMPLIANCE AND SOLVENCY

Select TWO actions that will ensure the legal compliance and two actions that will help the solvency of a business

Action	Legal Compliance	Solvency
Ensure financial statements are filed on time	✓	
Improve credit control procedures		✓
Maintain a petty cash book		
Create and maintain a cash budget		✓
Ensure the work place is a safe environment for staff and visitors	✓	

12   THE ACCOUNTING FUNCTION

The Accounting function is an essential part of the business. Select TWO actions for each of the columns. Actions should only be selected once:

Actions	Efficient running of the business	Solvency of the business	Legal Compliance
Monitor cashflow		✓	
Provide quotation to customer			
Ensure Sales Tax is paid to HMRC on time			✓
Regularly chase outstanding receivables		✓	
Ensure inventory is ordered when it falls to the minimum level	✓		
Ensure members of staff are first aid trained			✓
Regular maintenance of machinery	✓		
Produce a staff rota for tea making			

13 ISSUES

Which TWO of the following issues would you try to resolve yourself?

- The paper for the photocopier keeps running out without a new order being placed.

- Somebody in the office continues to prop the fire door open.

14 PETTY CASH

Identify the most likely effect on the organisation if you were unable to complete the petty cash reconciliation on time.

- Fraudulent activity may have taken place and go undetected

15 CONFLICT

Some issues may lead to conflict in the workplace. Indicate which issues can be resolved by you and which should be referred to your line manager.

Issue	Resolve myself	Refer to line manager
Your manager has asked you to complete a Statement of Financial position, however you do not have the accounting knowledge to do this		✓
You suspect your colleague knows your computer password	✓	
You suspect an expenses form which has been passed to you has non-business expenses on it and the form has been submitted by a manager		✓

LO2 USE PERSONAL SKILLS DEVELOPMENT IN FINANCE

16 CPD

(a) Identify TWO of the following activities that count towards an employee's continuing professional development requirements.

- Complete a course to further relevant knowledge

- Read articles online related to the trade in which the employee works

(b) Identify the strength, weakness, opportunity and threat from the information listed below.

	Strength	Weakness	Opportunity	Threat
Attend a time management course			✓	
Leaves filing to the end of the week		✓		
Excellent customer service	✓			
Insufficient staff members to cover time off for courses				✓

17 PERFORMANCE

Indicate which TWO courses would be appropriate for you to attend:

- Bookkeeping course

- Communication and presentation skills

Identify whether each of the following statements is TRUE or FALSE.

A qualified accountant does not need to attend Continued Professional Development courses — False

CPD must be undertaken for a minimum of 1 day per month — False

18 WEAKNESSES

(a) Your manager has assessed that you have the following weaknesses:

(1) Poor communications skills – Attend a 'how to communicate in an office' course

(2) Poor timekeeping – Adopt a new clock in and out system for the office

(3) Inadequate technical accounting skills – Attend a bookkeeping course

(b) Identify whether each of the following statements is TRUE or FALSE

All accountants, qualified and unqualified must complete CPD — False

CPD must be carried out on an annual basis by unqualified members — False

CPD must be carried out on an annual basis by qualified members — True

19 APPRAISAL

(a) **Identify whether each of the following statements is TRUE or FALSE.**

An employee performance appraisal is designed to focus solely upon weaknesses problems experienced by an employee during the appraisal period. — False

There is a benefit in an employee undertaking a self-appraisal exercise even if their employer operates a system of annual appraisal. — True

An appraisal is a 'backward looking process' that concentrates solely upon what has happened during the previous year. — False

An appraisal process should allow an employee the opportunity to identify and discuss aspects of their work that they have either performed very well or performed less well during the previous year. — True

An effective appraisal process should result in objectives or goals to be achieved during the following year. — True

20 SELF-DEVELOPMENT

(a) You currently work in the financial accounting department of your organisation and have identified the need for some self-development activities.

Identify the development activity from the picklist below that will help you to meet each of your self-development needs.

Self-development need	Development activity
To improve your practical experience of using the purchase ledger management system used by your organisation	Work shadowing of an experienced colleague who deals with management of the purchase ledger
To develop a better understanding of financial accounting theory, principles and techniques	Study for a professional accountancy qualification
To improve your knowledge of the goods and services provided by your organisation	Review the product catalogue of your organisation
To improve your knowledge and understanding of how the management accounting department compiles product costings	Request a brief secondment to the management accounting department to develop knowledge and understanding of product costing
To improve your communication and presentation skills in meetings	Attend a practical course for 'effective communication skills' course.

LO3 PRODUCE WORK EFFECTIVELY

21 (a) REGIONAL SALES

(a) What is the total sales figure for the quarter? **£690,000**

(b) What percentage of the total sales was made by the North (round your answer to 2 decimal places)? **23.19%**

(c) What percentage of total sales was made by the Eastern and Western regions (round your answer to 2 decimal places)? **55.07%**

(b) WIGGINS LTD

(a) What were the total sales for the first 3 months? **£1,377,292**

(b) What was the percentage increase from March to April? **0.76%**

(c) What will sales be in September 20X4 if they are 5% higher than August 20X4? **£495,912.90**

(d) How much higher (in £) are sales in June than March? **£6,259**

22   BOB

> From: bob@accountancyfirm.co.uk
>
> To: ally@accountancyfirm.co.uk
>
> Subject: AAT Exam Performance
>
>
> Hello Ally,
>
> I would like to discuss the above with you tomorrow afternoon. In particular I would like to review the performance of John Barnes with a view to finding out why he has performed poorly. I also hope we can resolve this issue by working together with John.
>
>
> Regards
>
> Bob

23   K KIPLING

> From AATstudent@Kaplan.co.uk
>
> To: kk@cakes4tea.org.uk
>
> Subject: Meeting confirmation
>
> Good morning Mr Kipling
>
> Following our telephone conversation I confirm the meeting which is to take place at your premises, on Monday at 2.30 pm.
>
> I will bring a copy of the business plan I have prepared.
>
> Kind regards
>
> Anna Howes

24   JOSHUA VALENTINE

> From: AATstudent@atoz.org.uk
>
> To: jvalentine@atoz.org.uk; cjenton@atoz.org.uk; dwheeler@atoz.org.uk
>
>
> Subject: Conference
>
>
> Hello All,
>
> This conference is being held at King's Hotel on Thursday at 10 am.
>
> The conference will be held regarding the issue of recycling within organisations.
>
> Please confirm your attendance.
>
> Regards,
>
> AAT Student

25   WORK SCHEDULE

Complete your to-do list for Monday in order of task completion.

(1)   Weekly planning meeting

(2)   Open and distribute post

(3)   Process sales invoices

(4)   Assist payroll manager

(5)   Frank post and take to PO

26   WORK PLANNING

Process payroll	5th
Bank reconciliation	3rd
Wages reconciliation	2nd
Overtime calculation	6th
Team meeting	1st
Cash to bank	4th

27   FEEDBACK

Select two conclusions that could be drawn from the feedback

- Most delegates found the venue difficult to find

- The course was relevant to the delegates' job role

Select two items which should be investigated

- Why was there so little feedback received

- Look for a different venue

28   SURVEY

(a)   How many people were asked each question? 60

(b)   In terms of work/life balance, are staff unhappy

(c)   In terms of current pay/ are most people happy

(d)   Do the majority of people agree that there are good promotion prospects – no

29   REPORT CONTENT

What information is usually contained within the areas of a report listed below?

	Introduction	*Appendices*
Information regarding what the report is based upon	✓	
Supporting calculations for figures contained within the body of the report		✓

LO4 CORPORATE SOCIAL RESPONSIBILITY, ETHICS AND SUSTAINABILITY

30 PRINCIPLES

The fundamental code of ethics set out five principles that a professional accountant is required to comply with. Two principles are objectivity and professional competence/due care. Select TWO other ethical principles from the list below.

B   Integrity

D   Confidentiality

31 COMPANY SHARES

Your father owns some shares in a company which your company audits. You have recently found out that the company is struggling. This is going to be announced publicly shortly and will have an adverse effect on the share price. Which TWO fundamental ethical principles prevent you from telling your father about this?

A   Confidentiality

B   Objectivity

32 TAX ADVICE

Your best friend has recently started up in business and really needs some tax advice. Because they know you are training to be an accountant they have automatically assumed you are the right person to give advice. Which fundamental ethical principle prevents you from advising your best friend particularly regarding the fact that it is tax advice that he is seeking?

D   Professional competence and due care

33 CLIENT DISCUSSION

You and a work colleague decide to go out for dinner after work. Whilst in the restaurant you start to discuss a client and the issues which this client is currently facing. Unbeknown to you the CEO of their major supplier is sat at the next table and hears everything which you have discussed. Which fundamental ethical principle prevents you and your colleague from discussing this in public?

A   Confidentiality

34 ACCOUNTING LEGISLATION

Your work colleague has decided not to comply with the relevant accounting legislation when preparing a client's account as they 'can't be bothered'. Which TWO fundamental ethical principles is your colleague in breach of?

C   Professional Behaviour

D   Professional competence and due care

35 FRAUD

You have recently discovered that your manager is committing fraud. Your manager suspects that you know, and have threatened you with termination of your contract if you decide to whistle blow him. Which threat to fundamental ethical principles are you faced with?

E   Intimidation

36 NEW CLIENT

Your company has recently taken on a new client and you have been asked to prepare the monthly management accounts. As soon as you start work on the accounts you realise that it is your Auntie's Company. Which threat to principles are you faced with?

C   Familiarity

37 3 Ps

What do the 3 Ps relate to in terms of balancing economic, environment and social needs?

C   Profit, People, Planet

38 SUSTAINABLE

Kapfin is looking to become more sustainable and a manager believes that she has come up with a few amazing suggestions. Which ONE of these suggestions relates to sustainability?

E   To look into the possibility of providing the AAT textbook via e-books instead of providing a paper copy to students

39 SUSTAINABILITY

Your friend is being encouraged to make a suggestion of how to improve sustainability within her workplace. Which ONE of the following suggestions should she put forward to her manager?

B   Look at installing motion sensor lights into the office block

40 SOLAR PANELS

A company is trying to improve sustainability and it is considering installing solar panels on the office roof to reduce their yearly electricity costs. However the initial costs of implementing this is 20% higher than originally budgeted for. From a sustainability perspective, should the company still pursue this even though it is going to have an adverse impact on cost?

A   Yes

41   CSR OBJECTIVESS

Review each of the practical situations below, and match each situation with the appropriate corporate social responsibility (CSR) objective from the drop-down menu. You may use a CSR objective more than once if required.

Practical situation	CSR objective
Your organisation has a policy of encouraging all members of the finance department study for an appropriate accountancy qualification and proving financial support for those who do so.	Ethical employment practices
Your organisation will shortly introduce 'paperless office' procedures whereby all customer orders are processed online and an accounting software package maintains the sales and purchase ledger accounts.	Environmentally-friendly policies
Your organisation issues a 'Corporate Policy of Ethical Practices' which it requires all potential suppliers to agree to before purchasing goods and services from them	Ethical business practices
Your organisation is currently installing lighting with movement sensors, so that lighting will automatically be switched off if no movement is sensed for 5 minutes. The lighting can be activated by movement only.	Environmentally-friendly policies
Your organisation has a policy, wherever practicable, of permitting employees to work flexible hours, including working from home.	Ethical employment practices

42   BENEFITS

(a)   Identify TWO benefits to the community from the list below if an organisation introduces corporate social responsibility policies.

A   Employee absence from work

B   Use of corporate resources to benefit the community

C   Employees using voluntary days of absence from work to support charitable activities.

D   Greater use of recycled materials.

(b)Identify TWO benefits to the environment from the list below if an organisation introduces corporate social responsibility policies.

A   Employee absence from work

B   Greater use of renewable resources to reduce waste

C   Employees using voluntary days of absence from work to support charitable activities.

D   Greater use of recycled materials

43   CORPORATE SOCIAL RESPONSIBILITY

Which THREE of the following initiatives will minimise the environmental impact of an organisation's business activities?

- Ensuring company cars purchased have high CO_2 emissions
- Offering free membership at a local gym
- Encouraging staff travel to work using public transport rather than using their cars
- Ensuring machines maximise energy consumption
- Installing energy-saving production equipment
- Asking staff to leave their computers on overnight
- Installing motion sensor lights which turn off when rooms are empty

44   EMPLOYEE WELFARE

Which THREE of the following initiatives will improve the welfare of employees in an organisation?

- Introducing flexible working conditions for staff
- Ensuring all staff complete at least 8 hours overtime per week
- Offering all staff training and support to those who wish to gain further qualifications
- Opening the office at weekends to allow staff to work on Saturdays and Sundays
- Providing an on-site gym for all staff to use
- Offering bonuses to senior management staff only

45   CORPORATE SOCIAL RESPONSIBILITY STATEMENTS

Identify whether each of the following statements is true or false.

Statement	True/False
Implementing corporate social responsibility initiatives incurs costs without benefits to the organisation.	False
An organisation can expect to receive both financial and non-financial benefits as a consequence of implementing corporate social responsibility initiatives.	True
Introducing corporate social responsibility initiatives should enhance the reputation of an organisation.	True
Corporate social responsibility policies may result in an organisation changing its production methods and/or changing its sources of materials supplies.	True

Section 6

ANSWERS TO PRACTICE QUESTIONS

ASSESSMENT OBJECTIVE 2

46   HLB WHOLESALE

(a)

<table>
<tr><td colspan="6" align="center">**Painting Supplies Ltd**
19 Edmund St
Newcastle, NE6 5DJ

VAT Registration No. 402 2958 02</td></tr>
<tr><td colspan="3">HLB Wholesale
98 Back St
Consett
DH4 3PD</td><td colspan="3">**Customer account code:** HLB24

Delivery note number: 46589

Date: 1 Feb 20XX</td></tr>
<tr><td colspan="6">**Invoice No:** 298</td></tr>
<tr><td>*Quantity*</td><td>*Product code*</td><td>*Total list price £*</td><td>*Net amount after discount £*</td><td>*VAT £*</td><td>*Gross £*</td></tr>
<tr><td align="center">20</td><td align="center">SD19</td><td align="center">300</td><td align="center">270</td><td align="center">54</td><td align="center">324</td></tr>
</table>

(b)

Trade discount

47 MASHED LTD

(a)

<table>
<tr><td colspan="6" align="center">**Hickory House**
22 Nursery Road
Keighley, BD22 7BD

VAT Registration No. 476 1397 02</td></tr>
<tr><td colspan="3">Mashed Ltd
42 Moorside Court
Ilkley
Leeds, LS29 4PR

Invoice No: 47</td><td colspan="3">**Customer account code:** MA87

Delivery note number: 472

Date: 1 Aug 20XX</td></tr>
<tr><td>Quantity of pots</td><td>Product code</td><td>Total list price £</td><td>Net amount after discount £</td><td>VAT £</td><td>Gross £</td></tr>
<tr><td>20</td><td>P10</td><td>100</td><td>90</td><td>18</td><td>108</td></tr>
</table>

(b)

Bulk discount

48 SDB

Sales day-book

Date 20XX	Details	Invoice number	Total £	VAT £	Net £	Sales type 1 £	Sales type 2 £
31 Dec	Poonams	105	3,600	600	3,000		3,000
31 Dec	D. Taylor	106	7,680	1,280	6,400	6,400	
31 Dec	Smiths	107	3,840	640	3,200		3,200
	Totals		15,120	2,520	12,600	6,400	6,200

49 WILLIAM & SAMMY LTD

(a)

Sales invoice 286

(b)

£4,481.28

(c)

£4,668.00

50 PIXIE PAPERS

Has the correct product been supplied by Pixie Paper?	Y
Has the correct net price been calculated?	N see N1
Has the total invoice price been calculated correctly?	N
What would be the VAT amount charged if the invoice was correct?	£90.00
What would be the total amount charged if the invoice was correct?	£540.00

N1 – the trade discount of 10% should have been deducted so that the net price was £450.

VAT @ 20% on the net price of £450 is then calculated as £90.00.

51 FREDDIE LTD

Purchases day-book

Date 20XX	Details	Invoice number	Total £	VAT £	Net £	Product 14211 £	Product 14212 £
31 July	Box Ltd	2177	960	160	800	800	
31 July	Shrew Ltd	2175	14,400	2,400	12,000	12,000	
31 July	Novot & Co	2176	4,800	800	4,000		4,000
	Totals		20,160	3,360	16,800	12,800	4,000

52 HOLLY LTD

(a)

Purchase return 286

(b)

£928.80

(c)

£172.00

(d)

£1,032.00

What would be the total amount charged if the invoice was correct?	£192.00

53 EP MANUFACTURERS

(a)

Cheque for £1,200

(b)

Invoice 488

(c)

£4,850.00

54   STANNY LTD

(a)

<table>
<tr><td colspan="3" align="center">**Ringo Rings**

37 Parker Lane

Stoke SK1 0KE

REMITTANCE ADVICE</td></tr>
<tr><td colspan="2">**To:** Stanny Ltd</td><td>**Date:** 31 Mar 20XX</td></tr>
<tr><td colspan="3">Please find attached our cheque in payment of the following amounts.</td></tr>
<tr><td>*Invoice number*</td><td>*Credit note number*</td><td>*Amount*</td></tr>
<tr><td align="center">694</td><td></td><td align="center">2,300</td></tr>
<tr><td align="center">658</td><td></td><td align="center">3,640</td></tr>
<tr><td></td><td align="center">198</td><td align="center">650</td></tr>
<tr><td></td><td align="center">154</td><td align="center">1,250</td></tr>
<tr><td></td><td align="right">**Total amount paid**</td><td align="center">**4,040**</td></tr>
</table>

(b)   A remittance note is for ours and the suppliers records   T

A remittance note is sent by a supplier confirming amounts
received from them   F

55   TOYWORLD

(a)

Cheque for £500

(b)

Invoice 505

(c)

£4,000

56   GREY GARAGES

Remittance advice

To: Mulberry Motors

From: Grey Garages

Payment method: BACS   **Date of payment:** 25 July

Items outstanding			Tick if included in payment
Date 20XX	Details	Amount £	
23-Jun	Invoice 213	740	✓
06-Jul	Credit note 14	120	✓
13-Jul	Invoice 216	620	✓
19-Jul	Invoice 257	870	
Total amount paid		£1,240	

57   ERRICO

Supplier	£	Date by which the payment should be received by the supplier
Giacomo	67.51	11 June 20XX
Gaetani	39.33	9 June 20XX

58   LADY LTD

General ledger

Purchases ledger control account

	£		£
		1 Dec Balance b/d	5,103.90
		18 Dec Purchases & Vat	**903.23**

VAT account

	£		£
		1 Dec Balance b/d	526.90
18 Dec PLCA	**150.53**		

Purchases account

	£		£
1 Dec Balance b/d	22,379.52		
18 Dec PLCA	**752.70**		

Subsidiary ledger

M Brown

	£		£
		1 Dec Balance b/d	68.50
		1 Dec PDB	**300.00**

H Madden

	£		£
		1 Dec Balance b/d	286.97
		5 Dec PDB	**183.55**

L Singh

	£		£
		1 Dec Balance b/d	125.89
		7 Dec PDB	**132.60**

A Stevens

	£		£
		1 Dec Balance b/d	12.36
		10 Dec PDB	**90.00**

N Shema

	£		£
		1 Dec Balance b/d	168.70
		18 Dec PDB	**197.08**

59   SPARKY LTD

(a)   What will be the entries in the sales ledger?

Sales ledger

Account name	Amount £	Debit ✓	Credit ✓
Clarkson Ltd	1,680		✓
Kyle & Co	720		✓

(b)   What will be the entries in the general ledger?

General ledger

Account name	Amount £	Debit ✓	Credit ✓
Sales ledger control account	2,400		✓
Sales returns	2,000	✓	
VAT	400	✓	

60   LOUIS LTD

(a)   What will be the entries in the sales ledger?

Account name	Amount £	Debit ✓	Credit ✓
Sheep & Co	3,840	✓	
Cow Ltd	11,760	✓	
Chicken & Partners	6,720	✓	
Pig Ltd	14,496	✓	

(b)   What will be the entries in the general ledger?

Account name	Amount £	Debit ✓	Credit ✓
Sales ledger control	36,816	✓	
VAT	6,136		✓
Sales	30,680		✓

61   THOMAS & TILLY

(a)   What will be the entries in the purchase ledger?

Purchases ledger

Account name	Amount £	Debit ✓	Credit ✓
May Ltd	1,920	✓	
Hammond & Co	1,200	✓	

(b)   What will be the entries in the general ledger?

General ledger

Account name	Amount £	Debit ✓	Credit ✓
Purchase ledger control account	3,120	✓	
Purchase returns	2,600		✓
VAT	520		✓

62   JESSICA & CO

(a)   What will be the entries in the purchases ledger?

Purchases ledger

Account name	Amount £	Debit ✓	Credit ✓
Iona Ltd	1,680	✓	
Matilda Ltd	4,320	✓	

(b)   What will be the entries in the general ledger?

General ledger

Account name	Amount £	Debit ✓	Credit ✓
Purchases ledger control account	6,000	✓	
Purchases returns	5,000		✓
VAT	1,000		✓

63   HORSEY REACH

(a)

Account name	Amount £	Debit ✓	Credit ✓
Sales ledger control	226.80		✓
VAT	37.80	✓	
Discounts allowed	189.00	✓	

(b)

Account name	Amount £	Debit ✓	Credit ✓
Ashleigh Buildings	36.00		✓
143 WGT	54.00		✓
McDuff McGregor	43.20		✓
Cameron Travel	93.60		✓

64   BUTTERFLY BEES

(a)

Account name	Amount £	Debit ✓	Credit ✓
Discounts received	356.00		✓
VAT	71.20		✓
PLCA	427.20	✓	

(b)

Account name	Amount £	Debit ✓	Credit ✓
Bella Bumps	24.00	✓	

65   OLIVIA ROSE BRIAL SUPPLIES

(a)

Account name	Amount £	Debit ✓	Credit ✓
Discounts allowed	189.00	✓	
VAT	37.80	✓	
SLCA	226.80		✓

(b)

Account name	Amount £	Debit ✓	Credit ✓
Bridezilla	54.00		✓

66 CHUGGER LTD

(a) General ledger

Account name	Amount £	Debit ✓	Credit ✓
Stationery expense	80	✓	
Repairs	200	✓	
VAT	56	✓	

(b) Sales ledger

Account name	Amount £	Debit ✓	Credit ✓
BBG Ltd	7,200		✓
EFG Ltd	5,000		✓

(c) General ledger

Account name	Amount £	Debit ✓	Credit ✓
Sales ledger control	12,200		✓

67 ITALIAN STALLIONS

(a) General ledger

Account name	Amount £	Debit ✓	Credit ✓
Office supplies	80	✓	
Repairs	160	✓	
VAT	48	✓	

(b) Sales ledger

Account name	Amount £	Debit ✓	Credit ✓
AAG Ltd	4,000		✓
HLG Ltd	3,000		✓

(c)   **General ledger**

Account name	Amount £	Debit ✓	Credit ✓
Sales ledger control	7,000		✓

68   FRED'S FISH

(a)   **Sales ledger**

Account name	Amount £	Debit ✓	Credit ✓
K and D Ltd	8,200		✓

(b)   **General ledger**

Account name	Amount £	Debit ✓	Credit ✓
Sales ledger control	8,200		✓

(c)   **General ledger**

Account name	Amount £	Debit ✓	Credit ✓
Stationery	100	✓	
VAT	20	✓	
Postage	800	✓	

69   ABC LTD

(a)   **Cash-book – credit side**

Details	Cash	Bank	VAT	Payables	Cash purchases	Repairs and renewals
Balance b/f						
S. Lampard	216		36		180	
S. Bobbins	264		44		220	
Penny Rhodes	530				530	
Henley's Ltd		4,925		4,925		
Epic Equipment Maintenance		480	80			400
Total	1,010	5,405	160	4,925	930	400

(b)   **Cash book – debit side**

Details	Cash	Bank	Receivables
Balance b/f	1,550	7,425	
D. Davies		851	851
E. Denholm		450	450
Total	1,550	8,726	1,301

(c)   £540 ($1,550 - $1,010)

(d)   £3,321 ($8,726 - $5,405)

(e)   Debit

70   BEDS

(a)   **Cash-book – credit side**

Details	Cash	Bank	VAT	Payables	Cash purchases	Repairs and renewals
Balance b/f						
A Blighty Ltd	708		118		590	
R Bromby	228		38		190	
Roxy Bland	230				230	
Burgess Ltd		2,400		2,400		
Fast Equipment Repairs		96	16			80
Total	1,166	2,496	172	2,400	1,010	80

(b)   **Cash book – debit side**

Details	Cash	Bank	Receivables
Balance b/f	1,175	3,825	
A Barnett		698	698
H Connelly		250	250
Total	1,175	4,773	948

(c)   £9 ($1,175 - $1,166)

(d)   £2,277 ($4,773 - $2,496)

(e)   Debit

71   HICKORY HOUSE

General ledger

Account name	Amount £	Debit ✓	Credit ✓
VAT	6.80	✓	
Postage	15.00	✓	
Motor expenses	12.40	✓	
Office expenses	21.60	✓	
Bank	90		✓

72   MESSI & CO

General ledger

Account name	Amount £	Debit ✓	Credit ✓
VAT	7.25	✓	
Postage	4.50	✓	
Motor expenses	8.00	✓	
Office expenses	28.28	✓	
Petty cash control	48.03		✓

73   YUMMY CUPCAKES

General ledger

Account name	Amount £	Debit ✓	Credit ✓
VAT	11.07	✓	
Sundry expenses	10.00	✓	
Business travel	45.37	✓	
Postage	4.00	✓	
Petty cash control	70.44		✓

74   BROOKLYN BOATS

Telephone

Date 20XX	Details	Amount £	Date 20XX	Details £	Amount £
01 Dec	Balance b/f	870	31 Dec	Balance c/d	1,220
12 Dec	Bank	350			
	Total	1,220		**Total**	1,220
1 Jan	Balance b/d	1,220			

Discounts received

Date 20XX	Details	Amount £	Date 20XX	Details £	Amount £
31 Dec	Balance c/d	600	1 Dec	Balance b/f	500
			15 Dec	Purchase Ledger control	100
	Total	600		**Total**	600
			1 Jan	Balance b/d	600

75   CRAZY CURTAINS

Electricity expense

Date 20XX	Details	Amount £	Date 20XX	Details £	Amount £
01 Jan	Bal b/f	200	31 Jan	Balance c/d	450
22 Jan	Bank	250			
	Total	450		**Total**	450
1 Feb	Balance b/d	450			

Rental income

Date 20XX	Details	Amount £	Date 20XX	Details £	Amount £
31 Jan	Balance c/d	1,000	01 Jan	Balance b/f	400
			28 Jan	Bank	600
	Total	1,000		**Total**	1,000
			1 Feb	Balance b/d	1,000

76   SMITH & SON

Account name	Amount £	Debit £	Credit £
Fixtures and fittings	8,250	8,250	
Capital	18,400		18,400
Bank overdraft	4,870		4,870
Petty cash control	350	350	
Sales ledger control (SLCA)	42,870	42,870	
Purchases ledger control (PLCA)	23,865		23,865
VAT owed to tax authorities	10,245		10,245
Inventory	9,870	9,870	
Loan from bank	22,484		22,484
Sales	180,264		180,264
Sales returns	5,420	5,420	
Purchases	129,030	129,030	
Purchases returns	2,678		2,678
Discount allowed	2,222	2,222	
Discount received	3,432		3,432
Heat and light	1,490	1,490	
Motor expenses	2,354	2,354	
Wages	42,709	42,709	
Rent and rates	10,600	10,600	
Repairs	3,020	3,020	
Hotel expenses	1,890	1,890	
Telephone	2,220	2,220	
Delivery costs	1,276	1,276	
Miscellaneous expenses	2,667	2,667	
Totals	532,476	266,238	266,238

77   EXPIALIDOCIOUS LTD

Account name	Amount £	Debit £	Credit £
Capital	25,360		25,360
Petty cash control	250	250	
Loan from bank	11,600		11,600
Sales ledger control (SLCA)	159,242	159,242	
Purchases ledger control (PLCA)	83,682		83,682
Motor vehicles	35,900	35,900	
Inventory	28,460	28,460	
Bank overdraft	10,063		10,063
VAT owing from tax authorities	15,980	15,980	
Purchases	343,014	343,014	
Purchases returns	1,515		1,515
Wages	56,150	56,150	
Motor expenses	2,950	2,950	
Interest income	400		400
Sales	532,900		532,900
Sales returns	5,760	5,760	
Stationery	1,900	1,900	
Light & heat	6,500	6,500	
Discount received	200		200
Discount allowed	2,160	2,160	
Interest paid on overdraft	550	550	
Travel	1,800	1,800	
Marketing	650	650	
Telephone	1,510	1,510	
Miscellaneous expenses	2,944	2,944	
Totals		665,720	665,720

Section 7

ANSWERS TO PRACTICE QUESTIONS

ASSESSMENT OBJECTIVE 3

78 INTREPID INTERIORS

(a)

Account name	Amount £	Debit ✔	Credit ✔
Cash at bank	7,250	✔	
Bank Loan	5,000		✔
Capital	10,625		✔
Motor vehicles	4,750	✔	
Insurances	575	✔	
Stationery	300	✔	
Sundry expenses	225	✔	
Motor expenses	135	✔	
Advertising	990	✔	
Rent and rates	1,400	✔	

(b)

Recording of a contra

79 DOWN & OUT

(i)

Account name	Amount £	Debit ✔	Credit ✔
Wages expense	9,567	✔	
Wages control	9,567		✔

(ii)

Account name	Amount £	Debit ✔	Credit ✔
HM Revenue and Customs	3,673		✔
Wages control	3,673	✔	

(iii)

Account name	Amount £	Debit ✓	Credit ✓
Bank	5,469		✓
Wages control	5,469	✓	

(iv)

Account name	Amount £	Debit ✓	Credit ✓
Trade union	425		✓
Wages control	425	✓	

Proof (not required to answer the question correctly):

Wages control

HM Revenue and Customs	3,673	Wages expense	9,567
Bank	5,469		
Trade union	425		
	9,567		9,567

80   RHYME TIME

(i)

Account name	Amount £	Debit ✓	Credit ✓
Wages expense	11,915	✓	
Wages control	11,915		✓

(ii)

Account name	Amount £	Debit ✓	Credit ✓
HM Revenue and Customs	5,026		✓
Wages control	5,026	✓	

(iii)

Account name	Amount £	Debit ✓	Credit ✓
Bank	5,739		✓
Wages control	5,739	✓	

(iv)

Account name	Amount £	Debit ✔	Credit ✔
Pension	1,150		✔
Wages control	1,150	✔	

Wages control

HM Revenue and Customs	5,026	Wages expense	11,915
Bank	5,739		
Pension	1,150		
	———		———
	11,915		11,915
	———		———

81 BEDROOM BITS

Account name	Amount £	Debit ✔	Credit ✔
Irrecoverable debts	2,000	✔	
VAT	400	✔	
Sales ledger control	2,400		✔

82 CHESTNUT

SLCA

Details	Amount £	Details	Amount £
Balance b/d	46,000	Contra	4,000
		Balance c/d	42,000
	46,000		**46,000**
Balance b/d	42,000		

PLCA

Details	Amount £	Details	Amount £
Contra	4,000	Balance b/d	31,000
Balance c/d	27,000		
	31,000		**31,000**
		Balance b/d	27,000

83   BEANZ

Account name	Amount £	Debit ✓	Credit ✓
Irrecoverable debts	4,350	✓	
VAT	870	✓	
Sales ledger control	5,220		✓

84   RENT ERROR

(i)

Account name	Amount £	Debit ✓	Credit ✓
Bank	500	✓	
Rent received	500		✓

(ii)

Account name	Amount £	Debit ✓	Credit ✓
Bank	500	✓	
Rent received	500		✓

85   GAS ERROR

Account name	Amount £	Debit ✓	Credit ✓
Gas expenses	300	✓	
Electricity expenses	300		✓

86   BUILDING ERROR

Account name	Amount £	Debit ✓	Credit ✓
Suspense	360,000	✓	
Bank	360,000		✓

87   SALES ERROR

Account name	Amount £	Debit ✓	Credit ✓
Sales	2,000	✓	
VAT	2,000		✓

88 CB INTERIORS

(i)

Account name	Amount £	Debit ✓	Credit ✓
Purchase ledger control	960	✓	

(ii)

Account name	Amount £	Debit ✓	Credit ✓
Purchase ledger control	9,600		✓

(iii)

Account name	Amount £	Debit ✓	Credit ✓
Suspense	8,640	✓	

89 ROGER DODGER

(i)

Account name	Amount £	Debit ✓	Credit ✓
VAT	1,680	✓	

(ii)

Account name	Amount £	Debit ✓	Credit ✓
VAT	1,320		✓

(iii)

Account name	Amount £	Debit ✓	Credit ✓
Suspense	360		✓

90 BUCKLEY DRAINS

(a)

Account name	Amount £	Debit ✓	Credit ✓
Suspense	10,805		✓

(b)

Account name	Amount £	Debit ✓	Credit ✓
Suspense	10,805	✓	
PLCA	10,805		✓

(c) Show one reason for maintaining the journal

	✓
To correct errors only	
To correct errors and record transactions that have not been recorded in any other book of prime entry	✓
To record transactions from every other book of prime entry.	

91 MENDONCA

(a)

Account name	Amount £	Debit ✓	Credit ✓
Suspense	1,980		✓

(b)

Account name	Amount £	Debit ✓	Credit ✓
Suspense	1,980	✓	
Wages	900	✓	
Bank	2,880		✓

91 BEASANT

(a)

Account name	Amount £	Debit ✓	Credit ✓
Suspense	15,000		✓

(b)

Account name	Amount £	Debit ✓	Credit ✓
Suspense	15,000	✓	
Sales	12,500		✓
VAT	2,500		✓

(c) Show one reason for maintaining the journal

	✓
To detect fraud	
To record non-regular transactions	✓
To record goods sold on credit	

93   HEARN

Journal entries

Account name	Debit £	Credit £
Rent	90	
Suspense		90
VAT	120	
Suspense		120

	Balances extracted on 30 June £	Balances at 1 July	
		Debit £	Credit £
Sales ledger control	34,560	34,560	
Purchases ledger control	21,420		21,420
VAT owing to HM Revenue and Customs	3,412		3,292
Capital	50,000		50,000
Sales	201,327		201,327
Sales returns	1,465	1,465	
Purchases	87,521	87,521	
Purchase returns	252		252
Plant and equipment	15,200	15,200	
Motor expenses	4,310	4,310	
Office expenses	10,321	10,321	
Rent and rates	21,420	21,510	
Heat and light	8,920	8,920	
Wages	53,205	53,205	
Irrecoverable debt	1,450	1,450	
Office equipment	42,030	42,030	
Bank overdraft	4201		4201
Suspense account (debit balance)	210		
Totals		**280,492**	**280,492**

94   RODMAN

Journal entries

Account name	Debit £	Credit £
Suspense	1,250	
VAT		1,250
Wages	8,600	
Suspense		8,600

	Balances extracted on 30 June £	Balances at 1 July	
		Debit £	Credit £
Sales ledger control	38,070	38,070	
Purchases ledger control	20,310		20,310
VAT owed from HM Revenue and Customs	2,510	1,260	
Capital	70,000		70,000
Sales	153,488		153,488
Sales returns	2,135	2,135	
Purchases	63,261	63,261	
Purchase returns	542		542
Plant and equipment	17,319	17,319	
Motor expenses	3,214	3,214	
Office expenses	6,421	6,421	
Rent and rates	17,414	17,414	
Heat and light	6,421	6,421	
Wages	45,532	54,132	
Irrecoverable debt	1,532	1,532	
Office equipment	35,313	35,313	
Bank overdraft	2,152		2,152
Suspense account (debit balance)	7,350		
Totals		**246,492**	**246,492**

94   LUXURY BATHROOMS

(a) – (c)

Date	Details	Bank	Date	Cheque	Details	Bank
01 April	Balance b/d	17,845	01 April	120045	R Sterling Ltd	8,850
19 April	Olsen & Lane	2,150	01 April	120046	Bert Cooper	2,250
22 April	Frith Ltd	685	01 April	120047	Hetko & Sons	64
22 April	Hodgetts & Co	282	02 April	120048	Barrett Ltd	3,256
04 April	Ricketts & Co	465	02 April	120049	K Plomer	542
			08 April	120050	I&E Brown	655
			08 April	120051	T Roberts	1,698
			14 April		AMB Ltd	2,265
			14 April		D Draper	2,950
			22 April		Bank charges	63
			23 April		Overdraft fee	25
24 April	Balance c/d	1,191				
		22,618				**22,618**
			25 April		Balance b/d	1,191

95   WHOLESALE FLOORING

(a) – (c)

Date 20XX	Details	Bank £	Date 20XX	Cheque number	Details	Bank £
			01 June		Balance b/d	5,125
16 June	Beeston's	550	01 June	104373	Good Iron	890
19 June	Airfleet exteriors	3,025	01 June	104374	Ashworth and Co	1,725
22 June	Jones's	2,775	01 June	104375	Ironfit	210
12 June	Aintree and Co	1,250	05 June	104376	OSS Ltd	1,275
			07 June	104377	Perfect Tools	725
			08 June	104378	Campden Ltd	784
			14 June	104379	Thornley and Thwaite	675
			14 June	104380	Castle and Cove	178
			20 June		MD County council	400
			23 June		Bank charges	160
23 June	Balance c/d	4,637	23 June		Overdraft fee	90
		12,237				12,237
			24 June		Balance b/d	4,637

97   MCKEOWN

(a) – (c)

Date 20XX	Details	Bank £	Date 20XX	Cheque number	Details	Bank £
01 June	Balance b/d	7,180	07 June	110157	Williams	430
12 June	Sherwood	640	07 June	110158	Forecast	520
14 June	Cash sales	1,200	07 June	110159	Beasant	1,240
22 June	Tweedy	860	07 June	110160	Davison	1,420
23 June	Butterwood	440	07 June	110161	Mildenhall	750
01 June	Interest received	85	23 June		Wilmott	300
20 June	Coyne	1,630				
23 June	Interest received	35				
			23 June		Balance c/d	7,410
		12,070				12,070
24 June	Balance b/d	7,410				

98   LUXURY BATHROOMS

Balance per bank statement	£82
Add:	
Name: Frith Ltd	£685
Name: Hodgetts & Co	£282
Total to add	£967
Less:	
Name: K Plomer	£542
Name: T Roberts	£1,698
Total to subtract	£2,240
Balance as per cash book	(£1,191)

99   WHOLESALE FLOORING

Balance per bank statement	(£9,584)
Add:	
Name: Airfleet Exteriors	£3,025
Name: Jones'	£2,775
Total to add	£5,800
Less:	
Name: Thornley & Thwaite	£675
Name: Castle & Cove	£178
Total to subtract	£853
Balance as per cash book	(£4,637)

100   MCKEOWN

(a)

Balance per bank statement	£8,770
Add:	
Name: Tweedy	£860
Name: Butterwood	£440
Total to add	£1,300
Less:	
Name: Beasant	£1,240
Name: Davison	£1,420
Total to subtract	£2,660
Balance as per cash book	£7,410

(b)

Balance carried down £	Bank column totals £
7,410	12,070

Workings: - Cash book

Date 20XX	Details	Bank £	Date 20XX	Cheque number	Details	Bank £
01 June	Balance b/d	7,180	07 June	110157	Williams	430
12 June	Sherwood	640	07 June	110158	Forecast	520
14 June	Cash sales	1,200	07 June	110159	Beasant	1,240
22 June	Tweedy	860	07 June	110160	Davison	1,420
23 June	Butterwood	440	07 June	110161	Mildenhall	750
01 June	Interest received	85	23 June		Wilmott	300
20 June	Coyne	1,630				
23 June	Interest received	35				
			23 June		Balance c/d	7,410
		12,070				12,070
24 June	Balance b/d	7,410				

101 MONSTER MUNCHIES

(a)

Details	Amount £	Debit ✓	Credit ✓
Balance of receivables at 1 June	48,000	✓	
Goods sold on credit	12,415	✓	
Receipts from credit customers	22,513		✓
Discount allowed	465		✓
Sales returns from credit customers	320		✓

(b)

Dr £37,117	✓

(c)

	£
Sales ledger control account balance as at 30 June	37,117
Total of subsidiary (sales) ledger accounts as at 30 June	36,797
Difference	320

(d)

Sales returns may have been omitted from the subsidiary ledger.	
Discounts allowed may have been omitted from the subsidiary ledger.	
Sales returns may have been entered in the subsidiary ledger twice.	✓
Discounts allowed may have been entered in the subsidiary ledger twice.	✓

(e)

Reconciliation of the sales ledger control account assures managers that the amount showing as owed to suppliers is correct.	
Reconciliation of the sales ledger control account assures managers that the amount showing as outstanding from customers is correct.	✓
Reconciliation of the sales ledger control account will show if a purchase invoice has been omitted from the purchase ledger.	
Reconciliation of the sales ledger control account will show if a purchase invoice has been omitted from the sales ledger.	

102 JACK'S BOX

(a)

Details	Amount £	Debit ✓	Credit ✓
Balance of receivables at 1 April	60,589	✓	
Goods sold on credit	26,869	✓	
Payments received from credit customers	29,411		✓
Discount allowed	598		✓
Goods returned from credit customers	1,223		✓

(b)

Dr £55,030	
Cr £55,030	
Dr £56,226	✓
Cr £56,226	
Dr £52,584	
Cr £52,584	

(c)

	£
Sales Ledger control account balances as at 30 April	56,226
Total of subsidiary (sales) ledger accounts as at 30 April	55,003
Difference	1,223

(d)

Sales returns may have been omitted from the subsidiary ledger	
Discounts allowed have been omitted from the subsidiary ledger.	
Sales returns have been entered into the subsidiary ledger twice	✓
Discounts allowed have been entered into the subsidiary ledger twice	

(e)

Reconciliation of the sales ledger control account will show if a purchase invoice has been omitted from the purchases ledger.	
Reconciliation of the sales ledger control account will show if a sales invoice has been omitted from the purchases ledger.	
Reconciliation of the sales ledger control account assures managers that the amount showing due to suppliers is correct.	
Reconciliation of the sales ledger control account assures managers that the amount showing due from customers is correct.	✓

103 ZHANG

(a)

SLCA

Details	Amount £	Details	Amount £
Balance b/d	65,830	SBD overcast	1,200
		Discount given	210
		Balance c/d	64,420
	65,830		**65,830**
Balance b/d	64,420		

List of balances:

	£
Total:	65,090
Contra missing	(800)
Credit note posted twice	130
Revised total:	64,420

(b) **Show whether the following statements are true or false:**

	True ✓	False ✓
An aged trade receivables analysis is used when chasing customers for outstanding payments.	✓	
An aged trade receivables analysis is sent to credit customers when payments are being requested.		✓

104 HANDYSIDE

(a)

PLCA

Details	Amount £	Details	Amount £
Returns	120	Balance b/d	25,360
		Missing invoice	720
Balance c/d	25,960		
	26,080		**26,080**
		Balance b/d	25,960

List of balances:

	£
Total	26,000
Net amount entered	400
Returns	(350)
Transposition error	(90)
Revised total	25,960

(b) **Show whether the following statements are true or false:**

	True ✓	False ✓
The purchases ledger control account enables a business to see how much is owed to individual suppliers		✓
The purchases ledger control account total should reconcile to the total of the list of supplier balances in the purchases ledger	✓	

105 RING RING TELEPHONE

(a)

VAT control

Details	Amount £	Details	Amount £
Sales returns	360	Sales	30,600
Purchases	16,200	Cash sales	48
		Purchases returns	1,160
Balance c/d	15,248		
	31,808		**31,808**
		Balance b/d	15,248

(b) No – it is £15,248 owed **to** HMRC

(c)

	£	Debit	Credit
Balance brought down	38,900	✓	

Workings:

VAT control

Details	Amount £	Details	Amount £
Debit balances	93,800	Credit balances	54,400
Purchase of equipment	400	Cash sales	900
		Balance c/d	38,900
	94,200		**94,200**
Balance b/d	38,900		

106 PHILIP'S CABINS

(a)

VAT control

Details	Amount £	Details	Amount £
Sales returns	600	Sales	35,960
Purchases	20,040	Cash sales	112
		Purchases returns	1,144
Balance c/d	16,576		
	37,216		**37,216**
		Balance b/d	16,576

(b) No – the amount owed to HMRC is £16,576.

107 DISLEY

(a)

	£	Debit	Credit
VAT total in the sales day book	65,420		65,420
VAT total in the purchases day book	21,340	21,340	
VAT total in the sales returns day book	480	480	
VAT balance brought forward, owed to HMRC	24,910		24,910
VAT on irrecoverable debts	830	830	
VAT on petty cash expenses paid	210	210	

(b) No – the amount owed to HMRC is £67,470.

(c)

	£	Debit	Credit
Balance brought down	19,730		✓

Workings:

VAT control

Details	Amount £	Details	Amount £
Debit balances	42,300	Credit balances	61,250
Irrecoverable debt	200	Discounts received	980
Balance c/d	19,730		
	62,230		**62,230**
		Balance b/d	19,730

108 AWESOME LTD

Task 1

Characteristic	FIFO	LIFO	AVCO
• Closing inventory is valued at £48,500.	✓		
• The issue of inventory is valued at £57,200.			✓
• The issue of inventory is valued at £66,900.		✓	

Task 2

	True	False
• FIFO values the issue of inventory at £47,500.	✓	
• AVCO values the closing inventory at £38,400.		✓
• LIFO values the closing inventory at £29,100.	✓	

109 AMAZING LTD

Task 1

Characteristic	FIFO	LIFO	AVCO
• Closing inventory is valued at £1,500.		✓	
• The issue of inventory is valued at £23,000.	✓		
• The issue of inventory is valued at £24,000.			✓

Task 2

	True	False
• LIFO values the issue of inventory at £26,500.	✓	
• AVCO values the closing inventory at £5,000.		✓
• FIFO values the closing inventory at £4,000.		✓

110 STONE LTD

Method	Cost of issue on 22 June	Closing inventory at 30 June
FIFO	£10,125 (500 × £15) + (150 × £17.50)	£17,200 (£8,750 + £4,950 + £6,125 + £7,500) – £10,125
LIFO	£11,450 (275 × £18) + (350 × £17.50) + (25 × £15)	£15,875 (£8,750 + £4,950 + £6,125 + £7,500) – £11,450
AVCO	£10,732 ((£7,500 + £6,125 + £4,950)/ (500 + 350 + 275)) × 650	£16,593 (£8,750 + £4,950 + £6,125 + £7,500) – £10,732

111 NATAL LTD

Task 1

Method	Cost of issue on 2 Dec	Closing inventory at 29 Dec
LIFO	£534,250 (50,000 × £7) + (14,000 × £8) + (8500 × £8.50)	£42,750 (£85,000 + £112,000 + £350,000 + £30,000) – £534,250
AVCO	£535,912 ((£85,000 + £112,000 + £350,000)/ (10,000 + 14,000 + 50,000)) × 72,500	£41,088 (£85,000 + £112,000 + £350,000 + £30,000) – £535,912

Task 2

	True	False
• FIFO would give a lower closing inventory valuation on the 29th December than LIFO and AVCO.	✓	
• FIFO would give a lower cost of issue on the 25th of December than LIFO and AVCO.		✓

112 GANDALF LTD

	Valuation £
• July 15	£1,030 **(500 × £1.70) + (120 × £1.50)**
• July 31	£660 **(200 × £1.80) + (200 × £1.50)**

inventory as total purchases (£4,750) less cost of issue

113 NULAB LTD

Payment method	Time-rate	Piecework	Piece-rate plus bonus
• Labour is paid based on the production achieved.		✓	
• Labour is paid extra if an agreed level of output is exceeded.			✓
• Labour is paid according to hours worked.	✓		

114 MANDELA LTD

Statement	True	False
• Time rate is paid based on the production achieved.		✓
• Overtime is paid for hours worked over the standard hours agreed.	✓	
• Piece rate is paid according to hours worked.		✓

115 PERRES LTD

Payment method	Basic rate	Overtime premium	Overtime rate
• This is the amount paid above the basic rate for hours worked in excess of the normal hours.		✓	
• This is the total amount paid per hour for hours worked in excess of the normal hours.			✓
• This is the amount paid per hour for normal hours worked.	✓		

116 TEVEZ LTD

Statement	True	False
• Direct labour costs can be identified with the goods being made or the service being provided.	✓	
• Indirect labour costs vary directly with the level of activity.		✓

117 BERDYCH LTD

Payment method	Variable	Fixed
• Labour that is paid based on a time rate basis per hour worked.	✓	
• Labour is paid on a monthly salary basis.		✓
• Labour that is based on number of units produced.	✓	

118 PIECEWORK STATEMENTS

Statement	True	False
• Piecework encourages employees to work harder.	✓	
• Piecework requires accurate recording of the number of hours staff have worked.		✓
• Piecework encourages workers to improve the quality of the units they produce.		✓

119 PHOENIX LTD

Statement	True	False
An employee who works 38 hours and makes 775 units will not receive a bonus.		✓
An employee who works 40 hours and makes 815 units will receive total pay of £342.50.	✓	
An employee who works 37 hours and makes 744 units will earn a bonus of £6.	✓	

120 KAHN LTD

Worker	Hours worked	Units produced	Basic wage	Bonus	Gross wage
A. Smith	35	175	£420	£0	£420
J. O'Hara	35	180	£420	£6	£426
M.Stizgt	35	185	£420	£12	£432

121   ENTERPRISE LTD

Worker	Hours worked	Basic wage	Overtime	Gross wage
J. Picard	37 hours	£420	£36	£456
B. Crusher	42 hours	£420	£126	£546
D. Troi	31 hours	£372	£0	£372

122   SGC LTD

Worker	Units produced in week	Gross wage
J. O'Neill	500 units	£660.00
S. Carter	650 units	£772.50

123   GOTHIC LTD

Worker	Hours worked	Units produced	Basic wage	Bonus	Gross wage
M. Shelley	37	300	£629	£20	£649
G. Leroux	37	312	£629	£80	£709
E. A. Poe	37	296	£629	£0	£629

124   AVENGERS LTD

Worker	Hours worked	Basic wage	Overtime	Gross wage
T. Stark	138	£1,380	£0	£1,380
B. Banner	142	£1,400	£25	£1,425
S. Rogers	145	£1,400	£63	£1,463

125   DRACO LTD

Worker	Units produced in week	Gross wage
P. Jones	240 units	£192
D. Bannatyne	350 units	£250
L. Redford	250 units	£200

126   JLA PLC

Statement	True	False
During a 30 hour week, an employee producing 192 units would receive a bonus of £16.	✓	
During a 35 hour week, an employee producing 240 units would receive total pay of £215.	✓	
During a 30 hour week, an employee producing 180 units would not receive a bonus.	✓	

127 INJUSTICE LTD

Worker	Units produced	Basic wage	Piece work	Gross wage
N. Wing	295	£175	£354	£529
W. Woman	355	£175	£426	£601
T. Flash	385	£175	£462	£637

128 GREENWOOD LTD

Worker	Hours worked	Units produced	Basic wage	Bonus	Gross wage
B. Ryan	35	175	£350	£0	£350
S. Chang	35	190	£350	£21	£371
E. Schneider	35	210	£350	£49	£399

129 DOOMSDAY LTD

Element	Total cost for 20,000 units	Unit cost
Direct costs	£1,250,000	£62.50
Production overhead	£75,000	£3.75
Non production overhead	£185,000	£9.25
Total costs	£1,510,000	£75.50

130 OLSEN LTD

Element	Total cost	Unit cost
Materials	£960,000	£12.00
Labour	£1,360,000	£17.00
Production overheads	£80,000	£1.00
Administration overheads	£40,000	£0.50
Total	£2,440,000	£30.50

131 CORONATION LTD

	Total cost for 5,000 units	Unit cost
Direct costs	£32,500	£6.50
Production overhead	£40,000	£8.00
Non production overhead	£45,000	£9.00
Total costs	£117,500	£23.50

132 LUTHOR LTD

Element	Unit cost
Materials	£60.00
Labour	£22.50
Fixed overheads	£38.00
Total	£120.50

133 WILKINSON LTD

Task 1

	Machine hour	Labour hour	Unit
Overheads (£)	150,000	150,000	150,000
Activity	10,000	12,500	60,000
Absorption rate (£)	15.00	12.00	2.50

Task 2

Cost	Machine hour (£)	Labour hour (£)	Unit (£)
Material	10.00	10.00	10.00
Labour	2.50	2.50	2.50
Direct cost	12.50	12.50	12.50
Overheads	2.50	3.00	2.50
Total unit cost	15.00	15.50	15.00

134 HODGSON LTD

Task 1

	Machine hour	Labour hour	Unit
Overheads (£)	250,000	250,000	250,000
Activity	15,000	20,000	100,000
Absorption rate (£)	16.67	12.50	2.50

Task 2

Cost	Machine hour (£)	Labour hour (£)	Unit (£)
Material	24.00	24.00	24.00
Labour	6.00	6.00	6.00
Direct cost	30.00	30.00	30.00
Overheads	5.56	6.25	2.50
Total unit cost	35.56	36.25	32.50

135 BARNES LTD

Task 1

	Machine hour	Labour hour	Unit
Overheads (£)	130,000	130,000	130,000
Activity	17,500	12,000	40,000
Absorption rate (£)	7.43	10.83	3.25

Task 2

Cost	Machine hour (£)	Labour hour (£)	Unit (£)
Material	15.00	15.00	15.00
Labour	5.00	5.00	5.00
Direct cost	20.00	20.00	20.00
Overheads	3.72	3.61	3.25
Total unit cost	23.72	23.61	23.25

136 ANDREW LTD

Task 1

	Machine hour	Labour hour	Unit
Overheads (£)	145,000	145,000	145,000
Activity	9,000	11,000	60,000
Absorption rate (£)	16.11	13.18	2.42

Task 2

Cost	Machine hour (£)	Labour hour (£)	Unit (£)
Material	8.00	8.00	8.00
Labour	7.00	7.00	7.00
Direct cost	15.00	15.00	15.00
Overheads	5.37	6.59	2.42
Total unit cost	20.37	21.59	17.42

137 JOKER LTD

Manufacturing account – Y/E 31 December

	£
Opening inventory of raw materials	50,000
Purchases of raw materials	120,000
Closing inventory of raw materials	65,000
DIRECT MATERIALS USED	
Direct labour	140,000
DIRECT COST	
Manufacturing overheads	85,000
MANUFACTURING COST	
Opening inventory of work in progress	48,000
Closing inventory of work in progress	52,000
COST OF GOODS MANUFACTURED	
Opening inventory of finished goods	57,000
Closing inventory of finished goods	61,000
COST OF GOODS SOLD	

	£
DIRECT MATERIALS USED	105,000
DIRECT COST	245,000
MANUFACTURING COST	330,000
COST OF GOODS MANUFACTURED	326,000
COST OF GOODS SOLD	322,000

138 RIDDLER LTD

Manufacturing account – Y/E 31 May

	£
Opening inventory of raw materials	14,000
Purchases of raw materials	100,000
Closing inventory of raw materials	20,000
DIRECT MATERIALS USED	**94,000**
Direct labour	194,000
DIRECT COST	**288,000**
Manufacturing overheads	106,000
MANUFACTURING COST	**394,000**
Opening inventory of work in progress	16,000
Closing inventory of work in progress	20,000
COST OF GOODS MANUFACTURED	**390,000**
Opening inventory of finished goods	60,000
Closing inventory of finished goods	50,000
COST OF GOODS SOLD	**400,000**

139 BOOKWORM LTD

Manufacturing account – Y/E 31 December

	£
Opening inventory of raw materials	5,000
Purchases of raw materials	15,000
Closing inventory of raw materials	8,000
DIRECT MATERIALS USED	**12,000**
Direct labour	15,000
DIRECT COST	**27,000**
Manufacturing overheads	25,000
MANUFACTURING COST	**52,000**
Opening inventory of work in progress	4,000
Closing inventory of work in progress	(6,000)
COST OF GOODS MANUFACTURED	**50,000**
Opening inventory of finished goods	12,000
Closing inventory of finished goods	(16,000)
COST OF GOODS SOLD	**46,000**

140 VARIOUS LTD

Statement	True	False
• A variance is the difference between budgeted and actual cost.	✓	
• A favourable variance occurs when actual costs are less than budgeted.	✓	
• An adverse variance occurs when actual income is less than budgeted.	✓	
• A favourable variance occurs when actual income is the same as budgeted income.		✓

141 JONES LTD

Statement	True	False
If budgeted sales are 6,000 units at £7.50 per unit and actual sales are £47,600, the sales variance is favourable	✓	
A favourable cost variance occurs when an actual cost of £9,800 is compared to a budgeted cost of £24 per unit for a budgeted output of 400 units		✓
A variance arises from a comparison of budgeted costs for last year with actual costs for this year		✓
If actual material costs are the same as budgeted costs for materials then no variance arises	✓	

142 LANCASTER LTD

Statement	True	False
If budgeted sales are 14,000 units at £3.50 per unit and actual sales are £45,200, the sales variance is favourable		✓
An adverse cost variance occurs when an actual cost of £68,400 is compared to a budgeted cost of £14 per unit for a budgeted output of 5,000 units		✓
A variance arises from a comparison of budgeted costs for this year with actual costs for this year	✓	
If actual material costs are the same as budgeted costs for materials then the materials variance is favourable		✓

143 GOODE LTD

Statement	True	False
The variance for the Direct Material cost of Department B should be reported to the purchasing manager	✓	
The variance for the Direct Labour cost for Department A should be reported to the sales manager		✓
The variance for the Direct Labour cost for Department B should be reported to the production manager of Department A		✓
A Direct Material cost variance that has been deemed Not Significant should not be reported	✓	

144 BROWN LTD

Statement	True	False
The variance for the Direct Material cost of Department A should be reported to the purchasing manager	✓	
The variance for the Direct Labour cost for Department A should be reported to the production manager of Department B		✓
The variance for sales should be reported to the sales manager	✓	
A Direct Material cost variance that has been deemed Significant should not be reported		✓

Direct labour	110,556	107,950	F	NS
Production overheads	14,190	12,500	F	S
Non-production overheads	16,190	17,880	A	S

145 BLUEBELL LTD

Cost type	Budget £	Actual £	Variance £	Adverse/ Favourable	%
Sales	£204,555	£197,455	7,100	A	3
Direct materials	£39,000	£42,300	3,300	A	8
Direct labour	£75,000	£83,000	8,000	A	11
Production overheads	£69,000	£64,800	4,200	F	6
Administration overheads	£53,000	£58,900	5,900	A	11

146 TRIUMPH LTD

Task 1

Statement	Fixed	Variable	Semi-variable
At 9,000 units this cost is £29,250, and at 12,000 units it is £39,000		✓	
At 5,000 units this cost is £5.20 per unit, and at 8,000 units it is £3.25 per unit	✓		
At 19,800 units, this cost is £64,500, and at 27,000 units it is £82,500			✓

Proof of variable and fixed costs:

£29,250 ÷ 9,000 units = £3.25, £39,000 ÷ 12,000 units = £3.25, therefore variable cost

5,000 units × £5.20 = £26,000, 8,000 units × £3.25 = £26,000, therefore fixed cost

£64,500 ÷ 19,800 units = £3.26, £82,500 ÷ 27,000 units = £3.06, therefore must be a **semi-variable** cost – it cannot be fixed (it changes as the number of units changes) and it cannot be purely variable as the cost per unit changes at different levels of activity.

Task 2

	6,000 units	7,000 units	10,000 units	14,000 units
Variable cost (£)	18,000			42,000
Fixed cost (£)	24,000			24,000
Total cost (£)	42,000	45,000	54,000	66,000

Using the hi-lo method:

For the volumes given, difference in costs = 54,000 – 45,000 = £9,000

Difference in volumes = 10,000 – 7,000 = 3,000 units

Therefore variable cost per unit = £9,000 ÷ 3,000 units = £3/unit

At 10,000 units, fixed costs = £54,000 – (10,000 × £3) = £24,000

147 BUNGLE LTD

Statement	True	False
Total variable costs will decrease.		✓
Total fixed costs will remain the same.	✓	
The variable cost per unit will remain the same.	✓	
The fixed cost per unit will increase.		✓

148 TF

Statement	True	False
Variable costs change directly with changes in activity.	✓	✓
Fixed costs change directly with changes in activity.		
Stepped costs are fixed within a set range of output.	✓	

149 GLACIER

Event performance report				
Cost	Budget (£)	Actual (£)	Variance (£)	Adverse/ Favourable
Licence cost	1,500	1,250	250	Favourable ▽
Funds				
Sponsorship funds raised	25,000	27,200	2,200	Favourable ▽

Note that the licence cost variance is favourable as the actual cost was less than the budgeted cost. The sponsorship funds raised exceeded the amount expected, and this variance is therefore a favourable variance.

150 BERLINE

Event cost performance report					
Cost	Budget (£)	Actual (£)	Variance (£)	Adverse/ Favourable	Significant
Refreshments	2,000	2,250	250	Adverse ▽	Yes ▽
Magazine	1,000	950	50	Favourable ▽	No ▽

Note that there is an adverse variance for the cost of refreshments. This is significant as the actual cost was more than 4% in excess of the budgeted cost. There is a favourable variance for the cost of producing the magazine. As this is a favourable variance, it does not need to be identified as significant. Only adverse variances of more than 4% are regarded as significant.

Section 8

ANSWERS TO PRACTICE QUESTIONS

AO4 COMMUNICATE FINANCIAL INFORMATION EFFECTIVELY

151   MRS MAY

> Hi Mrs May,
>
> Please find enclosed a copy of the invoice received from MayMe Ltd for a recent purchase.
>
> The unit price stated on the invoice is incorrect. The unit price wos quoted at £36 per unit on the purchase order, yet we have been invoiced £63 per unit.
>
> Pleaze credit this invoice and reissue with the correct amount of £36 per unit. One we have received the corrected invoice, we can make payment.
>
> Yours faithfully

152   BILLY

> Dear Billy,
>
> I was very cheesed to here that you did not receive your goods in proper working order. We have very strict internal procedures, which are designed to prevent faulty goods reaching our customers. Please rest assured that we are investigating fully you're case and are striving to ensure that this does not happen again in the future.
>
> By way of an apolojy we will be refunding you in full and offering you a 20% discount on your next purchase,
>
> Kind regards
>
> John Anderson
>
> Store manager

153 MR CADBURY

Dear Mr Cadbury

I enclose a copy of the invoice which **your** requested during **are** telephone conversation this morning.

Please note this invoice is dated **31** June and **therefor** is overdue for payment.

I look forward to receiving your cheque in full settlement by return of post.

Yours **faithfully**

154 JEEPERS LTD

(a)

Cost	Yes	No
• Materials used in production.	✓	
• Piecework labour costs.	✓	
• Salary of chief executive.		✓

(b)

Element	Unit product cost
Materials	£35
Labour	£8
Direct cost	£43
Overheads	£38
Total	£81

155 GLORIA LTD

(a)

Element	Unit cost	Total cost for 20,000 units
Variable production costs	£5.50	£110,000
Fixed production costs	£4.00	£80,000
Total production cost	£9.50	£190,000

(b)

During the meeting I will explain what a fixed production cost is, and provide an example of a fixed production cost. I will also explain what a variable production cost is, and provide an example of a variable production cos. I will then explain what a semi-variable cost is, and provide an example of a semi-variable cost. Finally, I will explain what happens to variable and fixed production costs if output increases from 20,000 units to 25, 000 units.

A fixed production cost is one that does not change with the level of output. An example of a fixed production cost is factory rent. Factory rent will not change, irrespective of whether output is 20,000 or 25,000 units.

> **A variable production cost** is one that changes with the level of output. An example of a variable production cost is the direct labour cost. For example, it may require two hours of labour at £12 per hour to product a unit of production.
>
> **If output increased from 20,000 units to 25,000** the fixed production cost (e.g. factory rent) will not change. However, the total variable production costs (e.g. direct labour cost) will change if output increases. Using the information in the previous paragraph, the total direct labour cost will increase by (2 hours × £12.00 × 5,000 units) £120,000.

156 BIZARRO LTD

(a)

Element	Unit cost	Total cost
Materials	£45.00	£765,000
Labour	£9.00	£153,000
Overheads	£2.50	£42,500
Total	£56.50	£960,500

(b)

> During the meeting I will explain what the different methods of paying employees, including providing an example of each method of pay.
>
> **Basic pay** is the payment made based upon hours worked. irrespective of what the employee actually does during those hours. For example, an employee may be paid at £250 per a standard working week of 35 hours, or a fixed salary of £1,000 per month.
>
> **Bonus pay** is an amount earned in addition to basic pay for achieving or exceeding a target. For example, a bonus of £5 per unit may be paid if an employee exceeds their weekly production target of 75 units per week. No bonus will be paid if the employee produced 75 or fewer units in a week.
>
> **Overtime pay** is an amount earned in addition to basic pay for additional hours worked in a given time period. Overtime is often paid at a premium rate in excess of the rate of basic pay. For example, An employee may be paid at a basic rate of £15 per hour for a 35-hour working week. If they work an extra 5 hours in excess of 35 hours in a specified week, they will be paid overtime at a rate of 'time and a half' for the additional hours. They would be paid at an increased hourly rate of £22.50 for the additional five hours worked.

157 VINNY LTD

Element	Unit cost	Total cost
Materials	£5.00	£100,000
Labour	£8.00	£160,000
Overheads	£5.00	£100,000
Total	£18.00	£360,000

158 DARKSEID LTD

Element	Unit cost
Materials	£3.50
Labour	£6.75
Fixed overheads	£2.42
Total	£12.67

159 EREBOR LTD

(a)

Cost type	Budget £	Actual £	Variance £	Adverse or favourable (A or F)
Sales	600,500	597,800	2,700	A
Direct materials	205,800	208,500	2,700	A
Direct labour	155,000	154,800	200	F
Production overheads	65,000	72,100	7,100	A
Administration overheads	58,400	55,200	3,200	F

(b)

Report to the Warehouse Manager

Methods of inventory valuation

This report explains the three different methods of inventory valuation

FIFO (first in, first out)

This method of inventory valuation assumes that the first units received are the first units used or issued from stores. Therefore, the inventory valuation will be based upon the cost of the most recently received items.

AVCO (average cost)

This method bases the inventory valuation upon the average cost of units received during the accounting period. A new average cost is calculated each time prior to an issue ur usage to accommodate any recent receipts into stores.

LIFO (last in, first out)

This method of inventory valuation assumes that the most recently received units are the first units used or issued from stores. Consequently, the inventory valuation will be based upon the cost of the oldest items.

---

160 BELEGOST LTD

(a)

	Budget £	Actual £	Adverse or Favourable (A or F)	Significant or Not significant (S or NS)
Sales	205,000	207,100	F	NS
Direct materials	75,150	78,750	A	NS
Direct labour	110,556	107,950	F	NS
Production overheads	14,190	12,500	F	S
Non-production overheads	16,190	17,880	A	S

(b)

Report to the Production Manager

Variances and their investigation

Introduction

This report explains what a variance is. It then goes on to explain why only significant variances may be investigated by an organisation.

Variance explanation

A variance is a difference between what was expected to occur and what has actually happened. This is usually resented in monetary terms, or as a percentage of the budgeted figure. A variance may be either favourable, e.g. when actual cost is less than budgeted cost or it may be adverse e.g. when actual cost exceeds budgeted cost.

Investigation of variances

Normally, a business will investigate only significant variances. This is because significant variances are an indication of possible significant issues that were not anticipated or expected when the budget was prepared. Following investigation, appropriate action can be taken to rectify the problem.

161 MORIA LTD

(a)

Cost type	Budget	Variance	Variance as % of budget	Significant or Not significant
Sales	45,100	4,214	9	S
Material	15,750	1,260	8	S
Labour	12,915	805	6	NS
Variable overheads	5,750	315	5	NS
Fixed overheads	8,155	1,011	12	S

(b)

Notes for meeting with colleague

Direct cost and manufacturing cost of a product

During the meeting I will explain what the direct cost of a product is and what the manufacturing cost of a product is.

The direct cost of production comprises the cost of all direct raw materials used during the production period, plus the direct labour cost for the production period. This will include materials and components used in the manufacturing process to produce the finish product, along with manufacturing labour costs.

The manufacturing cost of production includes the direct cost of production plus manufacturing overheads. Manufacturing overheads include items such as heat, fuel and power costs for the factory.

Section 9

MOCK ASSESSMENT QUESTIONS

Scenario: The tasks are set in a business situation where the following conditions apply:

- You are employed as an accounts assistant in the financial accounting function at MM Manufacturing (MM).

- MM uses a manual bookkeeping system.

- Double entry takes place in the general ledger. Individual accounts of trade receivables and trade payables are kept in the sales and purchases ledgers as subsidiary accounts.

- The cash book and petty cash book should be treated as part of the double entry system unless the task instructions state otherwise.

- The VAT rate is 20%.

TASK 1   **(12 marks)**

Your workload for the week has been prepared by your supervisor and is listed in the table below. Your hours of work are 9am to 5pm with an hour for lunch from 12.00 to 13.00. There is a compulsory staff meeting on a Monday afternoon at 1pm, which lasts for one hour. You are required to take the minutes of this meeting.

In the event of any clash of workload activities, priority should be given to the tasks which are performed on a daily basis.

Task	Task to be completed by:		Task Duration
	Day	Time	
Complete supplier payment run.	Thursday	14.00	2 hours
Perform supplier statement reconciliations	Wednesday	17.00	2 hours
Answer customer and supplier emails	Daily	12.00	1 hour
Bank reconciliation	Friday	17.00	2 hours
Process purchase invoices	Tuesday	15.00	3 hours
Prepare banking summary	Daily	10.00	1 hour
Process sales invoices	Mon & Thurs	17.00	2 hours each
Prepare sales invoices	Thursday	16.00	2 hours
Prepare bank payments information	Wed & Fri	16.00	2 hours each

Your supervisor has sent you the following email:

Hi,

I have been asked to prepare a report for senior management relating to the petty cash expenditure of the business, as it seems to be increasing quite dramatically. I require you to prepare an analysis of petty cash expenditure for the previous month, which should take no longer than 1 hour to complete. My meeting is at 16.00 on Wednesday afternoon and I require this information by 14.00 on Wednesday.

Thank you

(a) **Complete a to-do list for Wednesday in order of priority. If an activity takes more than one hour, it can be done in stages as long as the task is completed by the required time. Daily tasks should be prioritised ahead of other tasks. Identify any lack of time to complete the required tasks separately.** **(4 marks)**

To-do List – Wednesday	
	9.00 – 10.00
	10.00 – 11.00
	11.00 – 12.00
Lunch	12.00 – 13.00
	13.00 – 14.00
	14.00 – 15.00
	15.00 – 16.00
	16.00 – 17.00
Lack of time	

(b) **Identify on which day, and which hours, you will be busiest with routine tasks. If an activity takes more than one hour, it can be done in stages as long as the task is completed by the required time. Identify any lack of time to complete the required tasks separately.** **(4 marks)**

To-do List	
	9.00 – 10.00
	10.00 – 11.00
	11.00 – 12.00
Lunch	12.00 – 13.00
	13.00 – 14.00
	14.00 – 15.00
	15.00 – 16.00
	16.00 – 17.00
Lack of time	

(c) **Identify what you should do in the event that you find you have too many activities planned on the 'to-do' list prepared by your supervisor.** **(1 mark)**

Course of action	Tick as appropriate
Advise your supervisor at the end of the day that you could not complete all work that was in your 'to-do' list	
Try to complete all tasks within the available time, but don't be concerned if work is left uncompleted	
Panic about not completing work and decide to work part of your lunch-hour and/or work late in the evening	
Discuss your workload at an early stage with your supervisor to prioritise tasks within the available time	
Leave it to your supervisor to find out whether or not work has been completed when expected	

You realise that you have two petty cash receipts, one for the purchase of some stationery supplies from a local business at a cost of £23.50 plus VAT, and the other for purchase of office cleaning materials at a cost of £29.34 inclusive of VAT.

(d) **What will be the combined amounts included in your petty cash claim form to record the two transactions?** **(2 marks)**

Net amount	£	
VAT amount	£	
Total amount	£	

After you have claimed your petty cash claim, you are advised that there is still a balance of cash amounting to £27.74.

(e) **What will be the accounting entries required to record the amount required to restore the petty cash float to the imprest amount of £125.00?** **(1 marks)**

Item	Debit entry	Credit entry
Cash book	£	£
Petty cash	£	£

TASK 2 **(12 marks)**

1.2

Scenario:

In response to employee feedback, MM Manufacturing has recently recruited a new Head of Corporate Communications, Louise Hardy. She has decided to introduce a monthly newsletter, to which all departments will have the opportunity to contribute. Contributions to the newsletter could be work-related or may also include news of other articles such as publication and explanation of corporate policies.

You have been asked to contribute to the first newsletter on behalf of the financial accounting department to make suggestions that may help employees in other departments to understand the work of the financial accounting department.

(a) **From the list below, identify FOUR suggestions that may help employees in other departments to understand the work of the financial accounting department.**

(4 marks)

Monthly Newsletter Number 1

Suggestions to help employees in other departments to understand the work of the financial accounting department.

∇ Drop down list for task 1.2 (a):

Benefits:

Produce only a printed copy of the newsletter which is made available in the staff refectory
Introduce cross-departmental teams to deal with issues and policies which affect the organisation as a whole
Introduce a system of compulsory secondment of individuals to work in other departments, irrespective of the business needs and of the skills, qualifications and experience an individual may have
Quarterly meetings with departmental representatives to explain what information the financial accounting department requires from each department, and why that information is needed
There is no need to introduce additional communication between departments
Each department should nominate a 'lead person' who would liaise and communicate with a nominated member of the financial accounting department, with both individuals feeding back comments to members of their own department as necessary
Leave it to individual employees to contact the financial accounting department if they would like information on what the financial accounting department does.
Introduce a 'buddy' system to enable an individual to shadow a member of the financial accounting department, perhaps for a day, so that they can gain a better understanding of how the work of the financial accounting department interacts with their own department

Louise has now been working at MM Manufacturing for three months and has decided that all staff should have awareness of how their work may impact upon the financial solvency of the organisation. She would like the next edition of the monthly newsletter to focus on this topic and has asked you to prepare a list of actions that the financial accounting department could introduce to improve solvency.

(b) **From the list below, identify FOUR actions to help improve solvency by dragging them into the monthly newsletter.** **(4 marks)**

Monthly Newsletter
Suggested ways for the financial accounting department to improve solvency

∇ Drop down list for task 1.2 (b):

Suggestions to improve solvency:

Renegotiate credit terms offered to credit customers and shorten the agreed credit period
Maintain the maximum possible level of inventory for all products so that, if an order is received, it can be fulfilled immediately
Monitor inventory levels so that goods are only manufactured when customers have ordered goods
Renegotiate credit terms with credit suppliers and shorten the agreed credit period
Identify alternative suppliers who can supply the goods and services required at a reduced price, or will offer bulk-purchase discounts
Rent or hire items of equipment which ae used only occasionally, rather than purchasing them and leaving them unused for periods of time
Purchase new items of plant and machinery now for new products that the organisation intends to commence production of in two years' time
Retain items of plant and equipment that are no longer need, rather than selling them.

The finance director, Ed Stone, wants to introduce a new accounting system into MM Manufacturing and is selecting members of a project team to implement the new system. The new system will integrate the financial accounting and management accounting systems, along with payroll and inventory management. He would like you to be a member of the team and has asked you to propose four colleagues that you feel have the attributes to work well within the project team.

To help you decide you have made some notes about each member of staff, as shown below.

Name	Experience	Brief assessment of skills and attributes
Che	Management accounts and inventory	Popular member of the department with excellent communication skills. Recognised as an 'IT geek' by colleagues who use him to resolve IT problems.
Evita	All areas of the finance function	An employee of MM Manufacturing for almost 30 years. Senior financial accountant, who has also worked as a management accountant. A good technical understanding of accounting issues, but finds IT systems problematic.
Nicola	Trainee in all areas of the finance function	A new, but inexperienced, colleague as who has recently left college. She does appear to be a confident person and is settling in well as a member of the finance team. Limited practical experience and has not yet started studying for professional accounting exams.
Leon	Financial accounting and management accounting	Good knowledge of current systems and also has a general knowledge of management and financial accounting processes. He is highly organised with good written communication skills.
Faisal	All areas of the finance function	Tends to work on his own, although he does appear to be efficient and organised. Tends not to speak or communicate during staff meetings.
Imelda	Financial accounting and Payroll	Excellent verbal communication skills and is normally focussed upon completion of work tasks and activities with positive results. She is respected by colleagues for her 'can do' attitude.
Nelson	Financial and management accounting	Basic knowledge of financial and management accounts, communicates well with close friends, does not communicate well in wider departmental activities. Has no experience of MM Manufacturing outwith his accounting work.
Benito	Inventory and payroll	Good knowledge of payroll systems and was a key member of a previous IT implementation team. He has very strong verbal communication skills and also has experience of inventory management.

(c) **Identify the FOUR members of staff that would be most effective as part of the project team.** **(4 marks)**

Che [　　]   Evita [　　]   Nicola [　　]   Leon [　　]

Faisal [　　]   Imelda [　　]   Nelson [　　]   Benito [　　]

TASK 3   (12 marks)

You have received the purchase invoice below from a credit supplier. The supplier has agreed to allow a 5% bulk discount off the list price of £0.80 per item.

Carter & Co
91 Mercer Street, Monkchester, MK16 8ST
VAT Registration No. 478 9245 01
Invoice No. 0369

To: MM Manufacturing   18 June 20X8
      5 Liverpool Way
      Blayton BA42 5YZ

                                                 £

1,500 ... Product CD693 @ £0.80 each   1,200.00
VAT @ 20%   240.00
                                          ———
                                    1440.00
                                          ———

Terms of payment: Net monthly account

You notice that the invoice amounts are incorrect.

(a) **What should be the correct amounts of the invoice?** **(3 marks)**

Net £	VAT £	Total £

You have received another invoice from Carter & Co whose account code is CAR768. There was no bulk discount offered for this order but Carter & Co has offered a prompt payment discount. You are ready to enter this invoice into the appropriate daybook

---

Carter & Co

91 Mercer Street, Monkchester, MK16 8ST

VAT Registration No. 478 9245 01

Invoice No. 0375

To: MM Manufacturing   20 June 20X8
     5 Liverpool Way
     Blayton BA42 5YZ

	£
350 ... Product CD680 @ £0.65 each	227.50
VAT @ 20%	45.50
	273.00

Terms of payment: 4% discount for payment within 10 days of date of invoice

---

(b) **Complete the entries in the daybook below by:**

- **selecting the correct daybook title, and**

- **making the necessary entries.**   **(7 marks)**

Title	▽

▽ Drop down list for task 1.3 (b):

Discounts allowed daybook
Discounts received daybook
Purchases daybook
Purchases returns daybook
Sales daybook
Sales returns daybook

Date 20X8	Details	Supplier account code	Invoice number	Total £	VAT £	Net £	Product CD693	Product CD680
20 June	▽	▽	0375					

▽ Drop down lists for task 1.3 (b):

Details
Carter & Co
MM Manufacturing

Supplier account code
CAR768
CD693
CD680

You must now prepare a payment to the supplier for invoice 0375 in order to take advantage of the prompt payment discount offered.

(c) **What will be the amount paid and what is the latest date by which the supplier should receive payment?** **(2 marks)**

Amount to be paid £	Date by which payment should be received
	▽

▽ Drop down list for task 1.3 (c):

18 June 20X8
20 June 20X8
28 June 20X8
30 June 20X8
18 July 20X8
20 July 20X8

TASK 4 (16 marks)

Scenario

It is now 7 July 20X8 and you are reconciling the bank statement with the cash book as at 30 June. The bank statement shows a bank overdraft of £1,959 and the cash book shows a credit bank balance of £1,449

You have checked the bank statement against the cash book and made a note of the unmatched items, as shown below.

Unmatched items on bank statement:

- A direct debit payment to Blayton Council of £540
- A BACS receipt from Alpha Products of £620

Unmatched items in cash book

- A cheque from a credit customer, Acme Ltd, of £850
- A cheque sent to a credit supplier, Darke Supplies, of £260.

(a) **Show the entries needed to update the cash book by:** **(4 marks)**

- **selecting which TWO items will be entered in the cash book**

- **showing whether each item selected will be a debit or credit entry.**

Item	Enter in cash book	Debit entry	Credit entry
Blayton Council	☐	☐	☐
Alpha Products	☐	☐	☐
Acme Ltd	☐	☐	☐
Darke Supplies	☐	☐	☐

(b) **Complete the bank reconciliation statement as at 30 June 20X8.** **(6 marks)**

Bank reconciliation statement	£
Balance as per bank statement – overdraft	
Add: item to increase overdraft	
▽	
Less: item to reduce overdraft	
▽	
Balance as per cash book (CR)	

▽ Drop down list for task 4 (b):

Blayton Council
Alpha Products
Acme Ltd
Darke Supplies

Having just completed the bank reconciliation statement, you are aware that the bank overdraft is close to the agreed overdraft limit of £2,500. You estimate that payments to credit suppliers in July 20X8 are likely to be likely to be £4,500 and receipts from credit customers will be £3,600. In accordance with organisational policy the Head of Treasury Services, Joann Davis, is to be advised so that funds can be transferred from elsewhere to ensure that the bank account remains within its authorised limit. One of your colleagues has drafted the email below to Joann Davis (jdavis@MMManufacturing.com) from accounts@MMManufacturing.com.

(c) **Review the draft email and select SIX errors by clicking on each error. Errors may include incorrect amounts and words wrongly spelt, incorrectly used or that are technically incorrect.** **(6 marks)**

From:	accounts@MMManufacturing.com
To:	jdavis@MMManufacturing.com
Subject:	Bank account balance
Date	7 July 20X8

Hi Joanne

Following completion of July's bank reconciliation statement, I can advice you that I expect payments of £5,400 and receipts of £3,600 by the end of this month. On that basis I would suggest that some funds should be transferred from the back account to ensure that the account stays within the authorised limit.

If you require further information, please contact me.

Kind regards

Accounts Clerk

TASK 5 (12 marks)

Scenario

MM Manufacturing has developed a strong commitment to identify and introduce suitable Corporate Social Responsibility initiatives (CSR) with a particular focus upon sustainability. You have been invited to join a team that has been asked to compile a report which outlines the sustainability initiatives planned for the year ahead.

(a) Drag TWO appropriate statements to create the introduction to the Corporate Social Responsibility and Sustainability Report below. (2 marks)

	Statements
MM Manufacturing Corporate Social Responsibility and Sustainability Report	being a responsible business by requiring all employees to have a personal development plan which is reviewed annually
Introduction	being a responsible business by sourcing goods from suppliers who have a similar commitment to sustainability and who publish their sustainability policies
MM Manufacturing is committed to:	being a responsible business and paying all employees at least 5% in excess of the national minimum wage
	being a responsible business and minimising the adverse impact our activities have upon sustainability and the environment
	being responsible business by buying materials from suppliers without considering the impact our suppliers may have on sustainability and the environment

(b) Drag FOUR appropriate initiatives in the local community and wider society section of the Corporate Social Responsibility and Sustainability report below. **(4 marks)**

	Initiatives:
MM Manufacturing Products Corporate Social Responsibility and Sustainability Report	Ensuring that all employees are able to pursue further education opportunities and study for appropriate professional qualifications
Our commitment to improving the local community and wider society. **Initiatives planned that will directly impact on the local community and wider society:**	Developing links with local schools and colleges to offer work experience programmes to final year students
	Purchasing staff laptops and PCs that conform to current best practice for energy conservation
	Donating surplus office equipment to a local day care centre
	Permitting employees two days leave of absence each year to use for charitable purposes, such as volunteering at a local charity or school
	Holding a company meeting every six months which require all employees to travel to a central location from numerous locations throughout the UK
	Ensuring that the organisation maximises profits by any means, so that they can pay more tax on those profits
	Choosing a local charity to sponsor and support throughout the following year

In support of its current CSR commitment, MM Manufacturing instigated a project to install more energy efficient equipment in the packing and despatch department which was completed last month.

You have been asked by your supervisor to complete a budget report for the direct costs incurred on the project. The budget report must clearly indicate whether each variance is favourable or adverse, and whether any variance calculated is significant, that is in excess of 5% of budget.

Budget costs are to be calculated as follows:

Boxes and cartons   3,500 items @ 5.25 per item

Packing paper   500 rolls at £12.50 per roll

Actual costs have already been entered into the report.

(c) Complete the table below by:

- inserting the budget cost for boxes and packing paper

- inserting the variance for each cost

- selecting whether each variance is favourable or adverse

- selecting whether each variance is significant or not. **(6 marks)**

Cost	Budget £	Actual £	Variance £	Favourable /Adverse	Significant
		Budget report			
Boxes etc.		19,475		▽	▽
Packaging		6,065		▽	▽

▽ Drop down lists for task 5 (c):

Favourable	Yes
Adverse	No

TASK 6 (24 marks)

Scenario

You have been seconded to the management accounting department to cover for the illness of a colleague. Your temporary supervisor has asked you to assist in an exercise dealing with cost behaviour exercise for a new product. Although total costs have been estimated for projected minimum and maximum levels of output, she would like a clearer indication of cost behaviour for all levels of output, with a segregation of fixed and variable costs.

(a) Complete the table below by: **(12 marks)**

- inserting the variable costs for each level of output

- inserting the fixed costs for each level of output

- inserting total costs for 8,000 units and 12,500 units levels of output.

Units	3,000	8,000	12,500	15,000
Variable costs (£)				
Fixed costs (£)				
Total costs (£)	62,500			152,500

(b)   In the box below, write notes in preparation for a meeting you will have with your temporary supervisor, including: (12 marks)

- a brief introduction outlining the areas you will discuss

- an explanation of how fixed and variable costs behave as levels of output change, using your figures in (a) to illustrate your answer

- a re-calculation of the fixed costs you calculated in (a) above, assuming they increased by 5% and provide an explanation of the effect of this on total costs

- an explanation of the effect on the total cost per unit as levels of output increase if fixed costs increased by 10% whilst variable cost per unit remains unchanged.

Your notes must be sufficiently detailed, clearly written and well-structured as they will be a formal record of your meeting discussion.

TASK 7 (12 marks)

Scenario

You are preparing for the month end at MM Manufacturing. The following three accounts are an extract from the general ledger.

Discount allowed

Details	Amount £	Details	Amount £
Balance b/f	2,489	Journal	426

Purchases returns

Details	Amount £	Details	Amount £
Journal	1,977	Balance b/f	2,546

Office expenses

Details	Amount £	Details	Amount £
Balance b/f	1,357		
Cash	145		

(a) **What will be the entries in the trial balance?** (6 marks)

Account name	Amount £	Debit	Credit
Discount allowed		☐	☐
Purchases returns		☐	☐
Office expenses		☐	☐

You have now completed and totalled the trial balance, but find it does not balance. The credit column is £378 more than the debit column so you have opened a suspense account.

(b) **Will the opening balance in the suspense account be a debit or credit entry?**

(1 mark)

Debit ☐

Credit ☐

You have identified that the error in the trial balance arose as a result of posting the total of the sales daybook for the final week of June as £13,246 instead of £13,624 in the trade receivables control account ('TRCA'). The entry in the bank account was correct.

You have partially prepared journal entries to correct the error and clear the suspense account.

(c) **Complete each journal entry by inserting the appropriate amount in either the debit or credit column. Do NOT enter a zero in unused debit or credit column cells.**

(3 marks)

Journal to remove the incorrect entry

Account name	Debit £	Credit £
TRCA		

Journal to record the correct entry

Account name	Debit £	Credit £
TRCA		

Journal to clear the suspense account

Account name	Debit £	Credit £
Suspense		

The trial balance showed an amount for the trade receivables control account travel of £110,754 before the error was identified.

(d) **What will be the entry in the trial balance following the journal entries in (c)?**

(2 marks)

Account name	Amount £	Debit	Credit
TRCA		☐	☐

Section 10

MOCK ASSESSMENT ANSWERS

TASK 1.1   **(12 marks)**

(a)   Complete a to-do list for Wednesday in order of priority. If an activity takes more than one hour, it can be done in stages as long as the task is completed by the required time. Identify any lack of time to complete the required tasks separately.

(4 marks)

To-do List - Wednesday	
Prepare banking summary	9.00 – 10.00
Supplier statement reconciliations	10.00 – 11.00
Customer and supplier emails	11.00 – 12.00
Lunch	12.00 – 13.00
Petty cash analysis	13.00 – 14.00
Bank payments run information	14.00 – 15.00
Bank payments run information	15.00 – 16.00
Supplier statement reconciliations	16.00 – 17.00
Lack of time	

(a)   Identify on which day, and which hours, you will be busiest with routine tasks. If an activity takes more than one hour, it can be done in stages as long as the task is completed by the required time. Daily tasks should be prioritised ahead of other tasks. Identify any lack of time to complete the required tasks separately. (4 marks)

To-do List Thursday	
Prepare banking summary	9.00 – 10.00
Supplier payment run (1 of 2 hours)	10.00 – 11.00
Customer and supplier emails	11.00 – 12.00
Lunch	12.00 – 13.00
Supplier payment run (1 of 2 hours)	13.00 – 14.00
Prepare sales invoices	14.00 – 15.00
Prepare sales invoices	15.00 – 16.00
Process sales invoices (1 of 2 hours)	16.00 – 17.00
Lack of time	
Process sales invoices (1 of 2 hours)	1 hour

Note that sales invoices should be prepared before they can be processed.

(b) Identify what you should do in the event that you find you have too many activities planned on the 'to-do' list prepared by your supervisor. **(1 mark)**

Course of action	Tick as appropriate
Advise your supervisor at the end of the day that you could not complete all work that was in your 'to-do' list	
Try to complete all tasks within the available time, but don't be concerned if work is left uncompleted	
Panic about not completing work and decide to work part of your lunch-hour and/or work late in the evening	
Discuss your workload at an early stage with your supervisor to prioritise tasks within the available time	✓
Leave it to your supervisor to find out whether or not work has been completed when expected	

(d) What will be the combined amounts included in your petty cash claim form to record the two transactions? **(2 marks)**

Net amount	£	47.95
VAT amount	£	9.59
Total amount	£	57.54

(e) What will be the accounting entries required to record the amount required to restore the petty cash float to the imprest amount of £125.00? **(1 marks)**

Item	Debit entry	Credit entry
Cash book	£	£97.26
Petty cash	£97.26	£

TASK 1.2 (12 marks)

(a) From the list below, identify FOUR suggestions that may help employees in other departments to understand the work of the financial accounting department. (4 marks)

Monthly Newsletter Number 1

Suggestions to help employees in other departments to understand the work of the financial accounting department.

Introduce cross-departmental teams to deal with issues and policies which affect the organisation as a whole

Quarterly meetings with departmental representatives to explain what information the financial accounting department requires from each department, and why that information is needed

Each department should nominate a 'lead person' who would liaise and communicate with a nominated member of the financial accounting department, with both individuals feeding back comments to members of their own department as necessary

Introduce a 'buddy' system to enable an individual to shadow a member of the financial accounting department, perhaps for a day, so that they can gain a better understanding of how the work of the financial accounting department interacts with their own department

---

(b) From the list below, identify FOUR actions to help improve solvency by dragging them into the monthly newsletter. (4 marks)

Monthly Newsletter

Suggested ways for the financial accounting department to improve solvency

Renegotiate credit terms offered to credit customers and shorten the agreed credit period

Monitor inventory levels so that goods are only manufactured when customers have ordered goods

Identify alternative suppliers who can supply the goods and services required at a reduced price, or will offer bulk-purchase discounts

Rent or hire items of equipment which ae used only occasionally, rather than purchasing them and leaving them unused for periods of time

---

(c) Identify the FOUR members of staff that would be most effective as part of the project team. (4 marks)

Che	✓	Evita		Nicola		Leon	✓
Faisal		Imelda	✓	Nelson		Benito	✓

TASK 3 (12 marks)

(a) What should be the correct amounts of the invoice? (3 marks)

Net £	VAT £	Total £
1,140.00	228.00	1,368.00

(b) Complete the entries in the daybook below by:

- selecting the correct daybook title, and

- making the necessary entries. (7 marks)

Title	Purchases daybook ▽

Date 20X8	Details	Supplier account code	Invoice number	Total £	VAT £	Net £	Product CD693	Product CD680
20 June	Carter & Co ▽	CAR768 ▽	0375	273.00	45.50	227.50		227.50

(c) What will be the amount paid and what is the latest date by which the supplier should receive payment? (2 marks)

Amount to be paid £	Date by which payment should be received
262.08	30 June 20X8 ▽

TASK 4 (16 marks)

(a) Show the entries needed to update the cash book by: (4 marks)

- selecting which TWO items will be entered in the cash book

- showing whether each item selected will be a debit or credit entry.

Item	Enter in cash book		Debit entry	Credit entry
Blayton Council	✓		☐	✓
Alpha Products	✓		✓	☐
Acme Ltd	☐		☐	☐
Darke Supplies	☐		☐	☐

(b) Complete the bank reconciliation statement as at 30 June 20X8. (6 marks)

Bank reconciliation statement	£
Balance as per bank statement – overdraft	1,959
Add: item to increase overdraft	
Darke Supplies ∇	260
Less: item to reduce overdraft	
Acme Ltd ∇	850
Balance as per cash book (CR)	1,369

(c) Review the draft email and select SIX errors by clicking on each error. Errors may include incorrect amounts and words wrongly spelt, incorrectly used or that are technically incorrect. Note – items in bold denote errors (6 marks)

From:	accounts@MMManufacturing.com
To:	jdavis@MMManufacturing.com
Subject:	Bank account balance
Date	7 July 20X8

Hi **Joanne**

Following completion of **July's** bank reconciliation statement, I can **advice** you that I expect payments of **£5,400** and receipts of £3,600 by the end of this month. On that basis I would suggest that some funds should be transferred **from** the **back** account to ensure that the account stays within the authorised limit.

If you require further information, please contact me.

Kind regards

Accounts Clerk

TASK 5 (12 marks)

(a) Drag TWO appropriate statements to create the introduction to the Corporate Social Responsibility and Sustainability Report below. (2 marks)

MM Manufacturing **Corporate Social Responsibility and Sustainability Report**
Introduction
MM Manufacturing is committed to:
buying goods from suppliers who have a similar commitment to sustainability and who publish their sustainability policies and the results of applying those policies
being a responsible business and minimising the adverse impact our activities have upon sustainability and the environment

(b) Drag FOUR appropriate initiatives in the local community and wider society section of the Corporate Social Responsibility and Sustainability report below. (4 marks)

MM Manufacturing Products **Corporate Social Responsibility and Sustainability Report**
Our commitment to improving the local community and wider society.
Initiatives planned that will directly impact on the local community and wider society:
Developing links with local schools and colleges to offer work experience programmes to final year students
Donating surplus office equipment to a local day care centre
Permitting employees two days leave of absence each year to use for charitable purposes, such as volunteering at a local charity or school
Choosing a local charity to sponsor and support throughout the following year

(c) Complete the table below by:

- inserting the budget cost for boxes and packing paper

- inserting the variance for each cost

- selecting whether each variance is favourable or adverse

- selecting whether each variance is significant or not. (6 marks)

	Budget report				
Cost	Budget £	Actual £	Variance £	Favourable /Adverse	Significant
Boxes etc.	18,375	19,475	1,100	Adverse ∇	Yes ∇
Packaging	6,250	6,065	185	Favourable ∇	No ∇

TASK 6 (24 marks)

(a) **Complete the table below by:** (12 marks)

- **inserting the variable costs for each level of output**

- **inserting the fixed costs for each level of output**

- **inserting total costs for 8,000 units and 12,500 units levels of output.**

Units	3,000	8,000	12,500	15,000
Variable costs (£)	22,500	60,000	93,750	112,500
Fixed costs (£)	40,000	40,000	40,000	40,000
Total costs (£)	62,500	100,000	133,750	152,500

Proof of split of total cost:

Total cost at 15,000 units = £152,500 and total cost at 3,000 units = £62,500
Difference in total cost = variable costs = £90,000 spread over 12, 000 units
Variable cost per unit = £90,000/12,000 = £7.50

(b) **In the box below, write notes in preparation for a meeting you will have with your temporary supervisor, including:** (12 marks)

- **a brief introduction outlining the areas you will discuss**

- **an explanation of how fixed and variable costs behave as levels of output change, using your figures in (a) to illustrate your answer**

- **a re-calculation of the fixed costs you calculated in (a) above, assuming they increased by 5% and provide an explanation of the effect of this on total costs**

- **an explanation of the effect on the total cost per unit as levels of output increase if fixed costs increased by 10% whilst variable cost per unit remains unchanged.**

Your notes must be sufficiently detailed, clearly written and well-structured as they will be a formal record of your meeting discussion.

During the meeting I will discuss the behaviour of fixed costs and variable costs at different levels of output. I will also discuss the impact of an increase in fixed costs upon total costs. In conclusion, I will explain the effect of a 10% increase in fixed costs on the total cost per unit as levels of output increase.

Fixed costs do not change as the level of output changes. Using the cost information for the new product, fixed costs were calculated to be £40,000 and they do not change.

The variable cost was calculated as £7.50 per unit for the new product. As output increases, the total variable costs will increase by £7.50 per unit.

If fixed costs increase by 10% from the original calculation, then fixed costs will be £44,000. As before, they will remain unchanged if the level of output changes. Total cost will therefore increase by £4,000 for each level of output, and will consequently increase the total cost per unit. Note that the increase in total cost per unit will be smaller as the level of output increases. This is because fixed costs will be spread over a greater number of units produced.

TASK 7 (12 marks)

(a) **What will be the entries in the trial balance?** (6 marks)

Account name	Amount £	Debit	Credit
Discount allowed	2,063	✓	
Purchases returns	569		✓
Office expenses	1,502	✓	

(b) **Will the opening balance in the suspense account be a debit or credit entry?**
(1 mark)

Debit ✓

Credit ☐

(c) **Complete each journal entry by inserting the appropriate amount in either the debit or credit column. Do NOT enter a zero in unused debit or credit column cells.**
(3 marks)

Journal to remove the incorrect entry

Account name	Debit £	Credit £
TRCA		13,246

Journal to record the correct entry

Account name	Debit £	Credit £
TRCA	13,624	

Journal to clear the suspense account

Account name	Debit £	Credit £
Suspense		378

(d) **What will be the entry in the trial balance following the journal entries in (c)?**
(2 marks)

Account name	Amount £	Debit	Credit
TRCA	111,132	✓	☐

AAT AQ2016

SAMPLE ASSESSMENT 2

FOUNDATION SYNOPTIC ASSESSMENT

Time allowed: 2 hours

Scenario: The tasks are set in a business situation where the following conditions apply:

- You are employed as an accounts assistant in the finance function at SCM Products.

- The finance function includes the financial and management accounting teams.

- SCM Products uses a manual bookkeeping system.

- Double entry takes place in the general ledger. Individual accounts of trade receivables and trade payables are kept in the sales and purchases ledgers as subsidiary accounts.

- The cash book and petty cash book should be treated as part of the double entry system unless the task instructions state otherwise.

- The VAT rate is 20%.

TASK 1   (12 marks)

Each week you work Monday to Friday from 09.00 until 16.00, and you are required to take lunch between 12.00 and 13.00. Each finance period is four weeks in duration so you plan your work in a four-week cycle.

The work schedules below show the days when routine tasks must be completed and the amount of time each task takes to complete. It is very important that you complete the management accounts tasks by the end of the identified day and the financial accounts tasks by the day and time indicated.

Monthly work schedules – management accounts					
	Monday	**Tuesday**	**Wednesday**	**Thursday**	**Friday**
Week 1	Material cost report (1 hour)		Material cost report (1hour)	Budget report (1 hour)	Product cost analysis (1 hour)
Week 2	Labour cost report (2 hours)			Budget report (1 hour)	Product cost analysis (2 hours)
Week 3		Labour cost report (1 hour)	Process invoices (1 hour)		
Week 4	Data gathering (1 hour)	Labour cost report (1 hour)		Variance analysis (1 hour)	Cost coding (2 hours)

Weekly work schedule – financial accounts			
Task	**Task to be completed each week by:**		**Task duration**
	Day	**Time**	
Reconcile statements	Friday	13.00	1 hour
Contact customers	Tuesday	13.00	2 hours
Post cheques	Every day	11.00	1 hour
Contact suppliers	Monday	11.00	1 hour
Departmental report	Wednesday	12.00	1 hour
Departmental charges	Thursday	12.00	2 hours

You are planning your work at the start of the day on Friday of week 4. You are required to attend a one-hour departmental meeting at 14.00 and you have also been asked to complete a non-routine petty cash book task by 10.00. Both of these tasks are already included on your to-do list.

1.1

(a)   **Complete your to-do list for today, Friday of week 4. Refer to the management and financial accounts schedules and drag the tasks to be completed into the to-do list below.** **(5 marks)**

Note: **You should drag a task into the to-do list more than once if the task takes more than one hour to complete.**

Tasks:

Budget report	Lunch
Contact customers	Material cost report
Contact suppliers	Post cheques
Cost coding	Process invoices
Data gathering	Product cost analysis
Departmental charges	Reconcile statements
Departmental report	Variance analysis
Labour cost report	

Friday, week 4 to-do list	Time
Petty cash book	09.00 – 10.00
	10.00 – 11.00
	11.00 – 12.00
	12.00 – 13.00
	13.00 – 14.00
Departmental meeting	14.00 – 15.00
	15.00 – 16.00

(b) **Identify the week in which you are least busy with tasks from the management and financial accounts schedules.** **(1 mark)**

▽ Drop down list for task 1.1 (b):

Week number
Week 1
Week 2
Week 3
Week 4

The petty cash task in your to-do list requires you to begin by entering a petty cash payment of £31.62 including VAT into the petty cash book.

(c) **What will be the amounts entered in the petty cash book to record this transaction?** **(3 marks)**

Net amount	£	
VAT amount	£	
Total amount	£	

You must now balance the petty cash book. The petty cash book shows a debit total of £150.00 and a credit total of £98.67.

(d) **What will be the amount of the balance carried down?** **(1 mark)**

£ [   ]

(e) **What will be the entry in the petty cash book to record the cash withdrawn from the bank to restore the imprest level of £150?** **(2 marks)**

Amount £	Debit	Credit
	☐	☐

TASK 2 (12 marks)

1.2

Scenario:

SCM Products has recruited a new Head of Finance, Rajesh Kumar, who wants to improve performance within the finance function. He has decided to introduce a system of weekly bulletins, prepared by finance staff, highlighting key aspects of their work.

You have been asked to contribute to the first week's bulletin and have decided to focus on the importance of finance staff establishing good business relationships.

(a) From the list below, identify FOUR benefits of finance staff at SCM Products establishing good business relationships by dragging them into the weekly bulletin.

(4 marks)

Weekly Bulletin Number 1
What are the benefits of finance staff establishing good working relationships?

∇ Drop down list for task 1.2 (a):

Benefits:

To build trust which may result in better sharing of information
To develop customer confidence which may result in them remaining solvent
To create improved communication channels which may improve efficiency
To build a better reputation which may lead to suppliers offering less credit
To develop respect which may assist in resolving disputes
To create communications that are fit for purpose and always understood
To build loyalty from customers which may lead to improved sales
To develop supplier confidence and ensure they maintain confidentiality

Rajesh has now been working at SCM Products for two months and has decided finance staff should be more aware of how their activities impact on solvency. He wants this week's bulletin to focus on this topic and has asked you to prepare a list of actions to help improve solvency.

(b) **From the list below, identify FOUR actions to help improve solvency by dragging them into the weekly bulletin.** **(4 marks)**

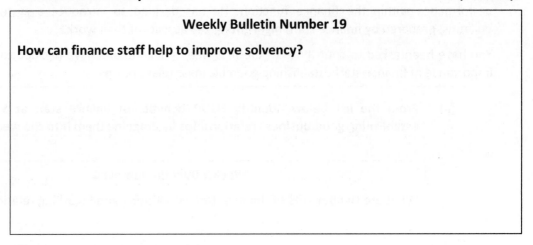

Weekly Bulletin Number 19

How can finance staff help to improve solvency?

∇ Drop down list for task 1.2 (b):

Benefits:

Extend the payment terms of all credit customers
Monitor bank balances and invest surplus funds
Monitor production output to ensure as many goods as possible are made
Negotiate low interest rates on amounts borrowed
Obtain credit where possible for all expenditure
Offer bulk discounts to maximise profit
Pay credit suppliers as late as possible without incurring penalties
Purchase a new vehicle for use by employees

Rajesh now wants to set up a project team of five staff to implement a new computer-based accounting system at SCM Products. He has said you will be part of the team and asked you to suggest four other members of staff that you feel have the attributes to work well within the project team.

To help you decide you have made some notes about each member of staff, as shown below.

Name	Experience	Brief assessment of skills and attributes
Bital	All areas of the finance function	Senior accountant, very knowledgeable, works primarily on his own, does not communicate well, finds IT systems challenging.
Zhe	Management accounts and cashiers	Popular member of the department, strong communication skills, good knowledge of the current IT system.
Borak	Financial accounts and Payroll	Valuable team member, great motivator, very focused on team objectives, strong verbal communication skills, popular with all staff.
Abdul	All areas of the finance function	Extremely quiet, works well on his own, completes tasks to a high standard, fails to appreciate wider team goals.
Jessica	Cashiers	Good knowledge of cashier procedures and general knowledge of finance systems, highly organised with good written communication skills.
Emily	Financial and management accounts	Basic knowledge of financial and management accounts, communicates well with close friends, does not communicate well in wider departmental activities.
Foday	Payroll	Good knowledge of payroll systems, key member of a previous IT implementation team, very strong verbal communication skills.
Simon	Trainee in all areas of the finance function	A new member of the team, first job since leaving school, limited knowledge of the finance department, lacks confidence, reluctant to communicate with colleagues.

(c) **Identify the FOUR members of staff that would be most effective as part of the project team.** **(4 marks)**

Bilal ☐   Borak ☐   Jessica ☐   Foday ☐

Zhe ☐   Abdul ☐   Emily ☐   Simon ☐

TASK 3   **(12 marks)**

You have received the invoice below from a credit supplier. The supplier has agreed to allow a 10% bulk discount off the list price of £0.75 per item.

Dawson Ltd

11 Hove Street, Grangeton, GX11 4HB

VAT Registration No. 398 4673 00

Invoice No. D1672

To: SCM Products   15 May 20XX
      14 London Road
      Parton, PA21 7NL

                                                                              £

1,200 ... Product D92 @ £0.75 each   900.00
VAT @ 20%   180.00
                                                                      _____

                                                                        1,080.00
                                                                      _____

Terms of payment: Net monthly account

You notice that the invoice amounts are incorrect.

(a)   What should be the correct amounts of the invoice: **(3 marks)**

Net £	VAT £	Total £

You have received another invoice from the same supplier whose account code is DAW322. There was no bulk discount offered for this order but the supplier has offered a prompt payment discount. You are ready to enter this invoice into the appropriate daybook

---

Dawson Ltd

11 Hove Street, Grangeton, GX11 4HB

VAT Registration No. 398 4673 00

Invoice No. D1676

To: SCM Products   17 May 20XX
      14 London Road
      Parton, PA21 7NL

                                                                              £

250 ... Product D87 @ £0.62 each   155.00
VAT @ 20%   31.00
                                                                      _____

                                                                          186.00
                                                                      _____

Terms of payment: 3% discount for payment within 10 days of date of invoice

---

(b) Complete the entries in the daybook below by:

- selecting the correct daybook title, and

- making the necessary entries. **(7 marks)**

Title	▽

▽ Drop down list for task 1.3 (b):

Discounts allowed daybook
Discounts received daybook
Purchases daybook
Purchases returns daybook
Sales daybook
Sales returns daybook

Date 20XX	Details	Supplier account code	Invoice number	Total £	VAT £	Net £	Product D87	Product D92
17 May	▽	▽	D1676					

▽ Drop down list for task 1.3 (b):

Details

Dawson Ltd
SCM Products

Supplier account code

DAW32
D1672
D1676

You must now prepare a payment to the supplier for invoice D1676 in order to take advantage of the prompt payment discount offered.

(c) What will be the amount paid and what is the latest date by which the supplier should receive payment. **(2 marks)**

Amount to be paid £	Date by which payment should be received
	▽

▽ Drop down list for task 1.3 (c):

15 May 20XX
17 May 20XX
25 May 20XX
27 May 20XX
31 May 20XX
30 June 20XX

TASK 4 (16 marks)

Scenario

You are reconciling the bank statement with the cash book at 30 June. The bank statement shows cash in the bank of £11,959 and the cash book shows a debit bank balance of £12,046

You have checked the bank statement against the cash book and made a note of the unmatched items, as shown below.

Unmatched items on bank statement:

- A direct debit payment to Central Insurance of £650

- A BACS receipt from Marl Motors of £706

Unmatched items in cash book

- A cheque from a credit customer, Devlin Dunn, of £433

- A cheque sent to a credit supplier, Sunil Ltd, of £290.

(a) **Show the entries needed to update the cash book by:** (4 marks)

- **selecting which TWO items will be entered in the cash book**

- **showing whether each item selected will be a debit or credit entry.**

Item	Enter in cash book		Debit entry	Credit entry
Central insurance	☐		☐	☐
Devlin Dunn	☐		☐	☐
Marl Motors	☐		☐	☐
Sunil Ltd	☐		☐	☐

(b) **Complete the bank reconciliation statement as at 30 June.** (6 marks)

Bank reconciliation statement	£
Balance as per bank statement	
Add:	
▽	
Less	
▽	
Balance as per cash book	

▽ Drop down list for task 4 (b):

Central Insurance
Devlin Dunn
Marl Motors
Sunil Ltd

Having just completed the bank reconciliation statement, you are aware of excess funds in the bank account. You estimate that payments to credit suppliers are likely to be £2,800 in July and £3,100 in August. In accordance with organisational policy the Chief Cashier, Susan Barnes, is to be advised that funds are available for investment and your colleague has drafted the email below to Susan Barnes (sbarnes@SCM.org.uk) from accounts@SCM.org.uk.

(c) **Review the draft email and select SIX errors by clicking on each error. Errors may include incorrect amounts and words wrongly spelt, incorrectly used or that are technically incorrect. You can remove your selection by clicking again** **(6 marks)**

From:	accounts@SCM.org.uk
To:	sbarnes@SCM.org.uk
Subject:	Bank Balance

Hello Suki

Following completion of June's bank rekonsiliation statement, I can confirm that there are surplus funds in the cash account. It is estimated that payments to credit customers are likely to be £3,800 in July and £3,100 in September. On that basis I would suggest that some funds are currently available for transfer into a high interest account.

If you require more details of estimated cash in and cash out, please do not hesitate to contact me.

Kind regards

Accounts Clerk

TASK 5 (12 marks)

Scenario

SCM Products is committed to improving its Corporate Social Responsibility (CSR) activities. You are part of a team that has been asked to assist in the preparation of an annual report detailing the CSR and sustainability initiatives planned

(a) Drag **TWO** appropriate statements to create the introduction to the Corporate Social Responsibility and Sustainability Report below. (2 marks)

	Statements
SCM Products **Corporate Social Responsibility and** **Sustainability Report**	being a responsible business and maximising the environmental impact of our activities
Introduction	buying goods in a manner that drives positive change within our industry
SCM Products is committed to:	being a responsible business and maximising our suppliers' profits
	being a responsible business by enabling the personal growth and fulfilment of our staff`
	buying materials at the lowest possible cost irrespective of the environmental impact of the materials

(b) Drag **FOUR** appropriate initiatives in the local community and wider society section of the Corporate Social Responsibility and Sustainability report below. (4 marks)

	Initiatives:
SCM Products **Corporate Social Responsibility and** **Sustainability Report**	Embedding a culture of CPD (Continuing Professional Development) and training into the workforce.
Our commitment to improving the local community and wider society.	Embedding a culture of commitment to volunteering within SCM Products.
Initiatives planned that will directly impact on the local community and wider society:	Ensuring the organisation uses the most energy efficiency delivery vehicles.
	Investing in projects to capture renewable energy sources.
	Facilitating employees' contributions to a charity of their choice.
	Providing interest free loans to all staff who wish to purchase a motor car.
	Providing opportunities for staff to work on raising funds to rebuild a day care centre near to the main offices.
	Providing opportunities for the unemployed to gain work experience.

In support of SCM Products' CSR commitment, a project to install more energy efficient equipment in the production plant was completed last month.

Your manager has asked you to complete a budget report for the direct costs spent on the project. The budget report must clearly indicate any variance that is significant, that is in excess of 10% of budget.

Budget costs are to be calculated as follows:

Materials   1,600 kilos @ £6.50 per kilo

Labour   500 hours at £12.50 per hour

Actual costs have already been entered into the report.

(c)   Complete the table below by:

- **inserting the budget cost for material and labour cost**

- **inserting the variance for each cost**

- **selecting whether each variance is significant or not.**   **(6 marks)**

Budget report				
Cost	**Budget £**	**Actual £**	**Variance £**	**Significant**
Material		11,645		∇
Labour		7,295		∇

∇ Drop down list for task 5 (c):

Yes
No

TASK 6 (24 marks)

Scenario

Your manager has asked you to assist in a cost behaviour exercise for a new product. Although total costs have been estimated for projected minimum and maximum levels of output, she wants a clearer indication of cost behaviour for all levels of output, with a segregation of fixed and variable costs.

(a)   Complete the table below by: (12 marks)

- inserting the variable costs for each level of output

- inserting the fixed costs for each level of output

- inserting total costs for 5,000 units and 7,500 units levels of output.

Units	2000	5000	7500	11000
Variable costs (£)				
Fixed costs (£)				
Total costs (£)	41000			105000

(b)   In the box below, write notes in preparation for a meeting you will have with your manager, including: (12 marks)

- a brief introduction outlining the areas you will discuss

- an explanation of how fixed and variable costs behave as levels of output change, using your figures in (a) to illustrate your answer

- a re-calculation of the fixed costs you calculated in (a) above, assuming they increased by 5% and provide an explanation of the effect of this on total costs

- an explanation of the effect on the total cost per unit as levels of output increase if fixed costs increased by 5% whilst variable cost per unit remains unchanged.

Your notes must be sufficiently detailed, clearly written and well-structured as they will be a formal record of your meeting discussion.

TASK 7 (12 marks)

Scenario

You are preparing for the month end at SCM Products These are three accounts in the general ledger.

Drawings

Details	Amount £	Details	Amount £
Balance b/f	1,190	Journal	125
Bank	250		

Bank interest received

Details	Amount £	Details	Amount £
		Balance b/f	342
		Bank	161

Office expenses

Details	Amount £	Details	Amount £
Balance b/f	3,462		
Cash	72		

(a) What will be the entries in the trial balance? (6 marks)

Account name	Amount £	Debit	Credit
Drawings		☐	☐
Bank interest received		☐	☐
Office expenses		☐	☐

You have now completed and totalled the trial balance, but find it does not balance. The credit column is £270 more than the debit column so you have opened a suspense account.

(b) Will the opening balance in the suspense account be a debit or credit entry?

(1 mark)

Debit ☐

Credit ☐

You have identified that the error in the trial balance has arisen from a bank payment of £636 for a rail fare being recorded in the travel account as £366. The entry in the bank account was correct.

You have partially prepared journal entries to correct the error and clear the suspense account.

(c) **Complete each journal entry by inserting the appropriate amount in either the debit or credit column. Do NOT enter a zero in unused debit or credit column cells.**

(3 marks)

Journal to remove the incorrect entry

Account name	Debit £	Credit £
Travel		

Journal to record the correct entry

Account name	Debit £	Credit £
Travel		

Journal to clear the suspense account

Account name	Debit £	Credit £
Suspense		

The trial balance showed an amount for travel of £1,589, before you discovered the error.

(d) **What will be the entry in the trial balance following the journal entries in (c)?**

(2 marks)

Account name	Amount £	Debit	Credit
Travel		☐	☐

AAT AQ2016

SAMPLE ASSESSMENT 2

FOUNDATION SYNOPTIC ASSESSMENT

Answers

TASK 1 (12 marks)

1.1

(a) Complete your to-do list for today, Friday of week 4. Refer to the management and financial accounts schedules and drag the tasks to be completed into the to-do list below. (5 marks)

Note: You should drag a task into the to-do list more than once if the task takes more than one hour to complete.

Friday, week 4 to-do list	Time
Petty cash book	09.00 – 10.00
Post cheques	10.00 – 11.00
Reconcile statements	11.00 – 12.00
Lunch	12.00 – 13.00
Cost coding	13.00 – 14.00
Departmental meeting	14.00 – 15.00
Cost coding	15.00 – 16.00

(b) Identify the week in which you are least busy with tasks from the management and financial accounts schedules. (1 mark)

Week number
Week 3 ▽

(c) What will be the amounts entered in the petty cash book to record this transaction? (3 marks)

Net amount	£	26.35
VAT amount	£	5.27
Total amount	£	31.62

(d) What will be the amount of the balance carried down? (1 mark)

£ | 51.33

(e) What will be the entry in the petty cash book to record the cash withdrawn from the bank to restore the imprest level of £150? (2 marks)

Amount £	Debit	Credit
98.67	✓	

TASK 2   (12 marks)

(a)   From the list below, identify FOUR benefits of finance staff at SCM Products establishing good business relationships by dragging them into the weekly bulletin.

(4 marks)

Weekly Bulletin Number 1
What are the benefits of finance staff establishing good working relationships?
To build trust which may result in better sharing of information
To create improved communication channels which may improve efficiency
To develop respect which may assist in resolving disputes
To build loyalty from customers which may lead to increased sales

(b)   From the list below, identify FOUR actions to help improve solvency by dragging them into the weekly bulletin.   (4 marks)

Weekly Bulletin Number 19
How can finance staff help to improve solvency?
Monitor bank balances and invest surplus funds
Negotiate low interest rates on amounts borrowed
Obtain credit where possible for all expenditure
Pay credit suppliers as late as possible without incurring penalties

(c)   Identify the FOUR members of staff that would be most effective as part of the project team.   (4 marks)

Bilal		Borak	✓	Jessica	✓	Foday	✓
Zhe	✓	Abdul		Emily		Simon	

TASK 3 (12 marks)

(a) What should be the correct amounts of the invoice: (3 marks)

Net £	VAT £	Total £
810	162	972

(b) Complete the entries in the daybook below by: (7 marks)

- selecting the correct daybook title, and

- making the necessary entries.

Title	Purchases daybook ▽

Date 20XX	Details	Supplier account code	Invoice number	Total £	VAT £	Net £	Product D87	Product D92
17 May	Dawson Ltd ▽	DAW32 ▽	D1676	186	31	155	155	

(c) What will be the amount paid and what is the latest date by which the supplier should receive payment. (2 marks)

Amount to be paid £	Date by which payment should be received
180.42	27 May 20XX ▽

TASK 4   **(16 marks)**

(a)   Show the entries needed to update the cash book by: **(4 marks)**

- selecting which TWO items will be entered in the cash book

- showing whether each item selected will be a debit or credit entry.

Item	Enter in cash book		Debit entry	Credit entry
Central insurance	✓		☐	✓
Devlin Dunn	☐		☐	☐
Marl Motors	✓		✓	☐
Sunil Ltd	☐		☐	☐

(b)   Complete the bank reconciliation statement as at 30 June.   **(6 marks)**

Bank reconciliation statement		£
Balance as per bank statement		11959
Add:		
Devlin Dunn	∇	433
Less		
Sunil Ltd	∇	290
Balance as per cash book		12102

(c)   Review the draft email and select SIX errors by clicking on each error. Errors may include incorrect amounts and words wrongly spelt, incorrectly used or that are technically incorrect. You can remove your selection by clicking again   **(6 marks)**

From:	accounts@SCM.org.uk
To:	sbarnes@SCM.org.uk
Subject:	Bank Balance

Hello **Suki**

Following completion of June's bank **rekonsiliation** statement, I can confirm that there are surplus funds in the **cash** account. It is estimated that payments to credit **customers** are likely to be **£3,800** in July and £3,100 in **September**. On that basis I would suggest that some funds are currently available for transfer into a high interest account.

If you require more details of estimated cash in and cash out, please do not hesitate to contact me.

Kind regards

Accounts Clerk

TASK 5 (12 marks)

(a) Drag TWO appropriate statements to create the introduction to the Corporate Social Responsibility and Sustainability Report below. (2 marks)

SCM Products Corporate Social Responsibility and Sustainability Report
Introduction
SCM Products is committed to:
buying goods in a manner that drives positive change within our industry
being a responsible business by enabling the personal growth and fulfilment of our staff`

(b) Drag FOUR appropriate initiatives in the local community and wider society section of the Corporate Social Responsibility and Sustainability report below. (4 marks)

SCM Products Corporate Social Responsibility and Sustainability Report
Our commitment to improving the local community and wider society. **Initiatives planned that will directly impact on the local community and wider society:**
Embedding a culture of commitment to volunteering within SCM Products.
Facilitating employees' contributions to a charity of their choice.
Providing opportunities for staff to work on raising funds to rebuild a day care centre near to the main offices.
Providing opportunities for the unemployed to gain work experience.

(c) Complete the table below by:

- inserting the budget cost for material and labour cost
- inserting the variance for each cost
- selecting whether each variance is significant or not. (6 marks)

Budget report					
Cost	Budget £	Actual £	Variance £	Significant	
Material	10400	11,645	1245	Yes	▽
Labour	6250	7,295	1045	Yes	▽

TASK 6   (24 marks)

(a)   Complete the table below by: (12 marks)

- inserting the variable costs for each level of output

- inserting the fixed costs for each level of output

- inserting total costs for 5,000 units and 7,500 units levels of output.

Units	2000	5000	7500	11000
Variable costs (£)	24000	40000	60000	88000
Fixed costs (£)	17000	17000	17000	17000
Total costs (£)	41000	57000	77000	105000

(b)   In the box below, write notes in preparation for a meeting you will have with your manager, including: (12 marks)

- a brief introduction outlining the areas you will discuss

- an explanation of how fixed and variable costs behave as levels of output change, using your figures in (a) to illustrate your answer

- a re-calculation of the fixed costs you calculated in (a) above, assuming they increased by 5% and provide an explanation of the effect of this on total costs

- an explanation of the effect on the total cost per unit as levels of output increase if fixed costs increased by 5% whilst variable cost per unit remains unchanged.

Your notes must be sufficiently detailed, clearly written and well structured as they will be a formal record of your meeting discussion.

During the meeting I will discuss the behaviours of fixed and variable costs as levels of output change, a re-calculation of fixed costs assuming a 5% increase in costs and the effect this will have on total costs. Finally I will explain the effect of a 5% increase in fixed costs on the total cost per unit as levels of output increase.

As the name suggests fixed costs remain constant irrespective of the levels of output. For example when 3000 units are produced the fixed costs were the same as when 11000 units were produced. Variable costs change dependent upon the levels of output. As the level of output increases then the variable costs also increase proportionately dependent upon the level of output.

Fixed costs will increase by £850 to £17,850. As fixed costs have increased by £850, total costs will increase by the same amount.

The unit costs will also increase as levels of output increase although the increase per unit will reduce as output increases. This is because the increase is spread out over more units.

TASK 7 (12 marks)

(a) **What will be the entries in the trial balance?** (6 marks)

Account name	Amount £	Debit	Credit
Drawings	1315	✔	
Bank interest received	503		✔
Office expenses	3534	✔	

(b) **Will the opening balance in the suspense account be a debit or credit entry?**

(1 mark)

Debit ✔

Credit ☐

(c) **Complete each journal entry by inserting the appropriate amount in either the debit or credit column. Do NOT enter a zero in unused debit or credit column cells.**

(3 marks)

Journal to remove the incorrect entry

Account name	Debit £	Credit £
Travel		366

Journal to record the correct entry

Account name	Debit £	Credit £
Travel	636	

Journal to clear the suspense account

Account name	Debit £	Credit £
Suspense		270

(d) **What will be the entry in the trial balance following the journal entries in (c)?**

(2 marks)

Account name	Amount £	Debit	Credit
Travel	1859	✔